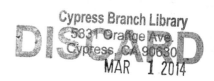

Living
HISTORY

Life in the North During the Civil War

Jim Whiting

ReferencePoint
Press®

San Diego, CA

© 2014 ReferencePoint Press, Inc.
Printed in the United States

For more information, contact:
ReferencePoint Press, Inc.
PO Box 27779
San Diego, CA 92198
www.ReferencePointPress.com

LIBRARY OF CONGRESS CATALOGING-IN-PUBLICATION DATA

Whiting, Jim, 1943-
  Life in the North during the Civil War / by Jim Whiting.
    pages cm. -- (Living history series)
  Includes bibliographical references and index.
  ISBN-13: 978-1-60152-576-5 (hardback)
  ISBN-10: 1-60152-576-1 (hardback)
  1. United States--History--Civil War, 1861-1865--Social aspects--Juvenile literature. 2. Northeastern States--Social conditions--19th century--Juvenile literature. 3. United States--Social conditions--To 1865--Juvenile literature. I. Title.
  E468.9.W54 2014
  973.7'1--dc23
                                                                            2012050549

Contents

Foreword

History is a complex and multifaceted discipline that embraces many different areas of human activity. Given the expansive possibilities for the study of history, it is significant that since the advent of formal writing in the Ancient Near East over six thousand years ago, the contents of most nonfiction historical literature have been overwhelmingly limited to politics, religion, warfare, and diplomacy.

Beginning in the 1960s, however, the focus of many historical works experienced a substantive change worldwide. This change resulted from the efforts and influence of an ever-increasing number of progressive contemporary historians who were entering the halls of academia. This new breed of academician, soon accompanied by many popular writers, argued for a major revision of the study of history, one in which the past would be presented from the ground up. What this meant was that the needs, wants, and thinking of ordinary people should and would become an integral part of the human record. As British historian Mary Fulbrook wrote in her 2005 book, *The People's State: East German Society from Hitler to Honecker,* students should be able to view "history with the people put back in." This approach to understanding the lives and times of people of the past has come to be known as social history. According to contemporary social historians, national and international affairs should be viewed not only from the perspective of those empowered to create policy but also through the eyes of those over whom power is exercised.

The American historian and best-selling author, Louis "Studs" Terkel, was one of the pioneers in the field of social history. He is best remembered for his oral histories, which were firsthand accounts of everyday life drawn from the recollections of interviewees who lived during pivotal events or periods in history. Terkel's first book, *Division Street America* (published in 1967), focuses on urban living in and around Chicago and is a compilation of seventy interviews of immigrants and native-born Americans. It was followed by several other oral histories including *Hard Times* (the 1930s depression), *Working* (people's feelings about their jobs), and his 1985 Pulitzer Prize–winning *The Good War* (about life in America before, during, and after World War II).

In keeping with contemporary efforts to present history by people and about people, ReferencePoint's *Living History* series offers students a journey through recorded history as recounted by those who lived it. While modern sources such as those found in *The Good War* and on radio and TV interviews are readily available, those dating to earlier periods in history are scarcer and often more obscure the further back in time one investigates. These important primary sources are there nonetheless waiting to be discovered in literary formats such as posters, letters, and diaries, and in artifacts such as vases, coins, and tombstones. And they are also found in places as varied as ancient Mesopotamia, Charles Dickens's England, and Nazi concentration camps. The *Living History* series uncovers these and other available sources as they relate the "living history" of real people to their student readers.

Important Events

1852
Harriet Beecher Stowe publishes *Uncle Tom's Cabin*, a landmark novel that converts untold numbers of Americans to the anti-slavery cause.

1861
Southern forces fire on Fort Sumter, marking the opening of hostilities in the Civil War; Confederate troops decisively defeat Union forces at the First Battle of Bull Run; Congress passes the Crittenden Resolution, affirming that the war aim of the North is to maintain the Union, not free the slaves.

1858
Incumbent senator Stephen Douglas and challenger Abraham Lincoln take part in a series of formal public debates in the Illinois Senate race. Lincoln loses the election, but the debates launch him into national prominence and eventually lead to his election as president.

1854   1856   1858   1860   1862

1857
The *Dred Scott* decision by the US Supreme Court denies American citizenship to slaves and their descendants.

1862
Lincoln calls for an additional three hundred thousand Union troops, with three-year terms of enlistment; Congress passes laws that allow blacks to join the Union army; the Battle of Antietam marks the bloodiest single day of the war and ends in a strategic Union victory, paving the way for Lincoln to issue the preliminary Emancipation Proclamation.

1859
Abolitionist John Brown leads a raid on the federal armory at Harpers Ferry, Virginia, hoping to provoke a slave uprising; he is captured and hanged.

1860
The election of Lincoln results in the secession of South Carolina from the Union on December 20, with ten other states following in the next six months.

of the Civil War

1863
The Emancipation Proclamation goes into effect, freeing all the slaves in the South; Congress passes a conscription act, requiring most able-bodied men in the North to sign up for military service; the Battle of Gettysburg turns back Confederate general Robert E. Lee's attempt to invade the North; draft riots in New York City result in more than one hundred deaths.

1864
General William T. Sherman captures Atlanta, Georgia, after months of campaigning; the victory boosts Northern morale and helps ensure Lincoln's reelection.

1866
Congress passes the Civil Rights Act, which extends citizenship and other rights to former slaves.

1875
Congress passes an act forbidding discrimination against blacks in public places.

1864	1866	1868	1870	1872

1867
Congress passes the first of the Reconstruction Acts, which sends federal troops into former Confederate States to enforce its terms.

1870
The Fifteenth Amendment, which guarantees blacks the right to vote, becomes law after being ratified by the states.

1877
Federal troops in the South are withdrawn, ending Reconstruction and allowing racism to flourish.

1865
Congress passes the Thirteenth Amendment, which calls for the abolition of slavery in the United States, and sends it to the states for their approval; Confederate general Robert E. Lee surrenders to Union general Ulysses S. Grant to effectively end the Civil War; Lincoln is assassinated; the Thirteenth Amendment is formally adopted.

Starting with Many Advantages

On April 20, 1861, perhaps half a million New Yorkers packed the streets leading into Union Square in downtown Manhattan. Eight days earlier, gunners from the new Confederate States of America had opened fire on the federal fortress of Fort Sumter, located in the harbor of Charleston, South Carolina. Unable to defend themselves, the handful of Union soldiers soon surrendered.

Now all these New Yorkers were responding to the threat to the Union with a mixture of anger and patriotism. As historian Adam Goodheart notes:

> If you were there among them that day, the thing that you would never forget—not even if you lived to see the next century—was the flags. The Stars and Stripes flew above the doors of department stores and town houses, from Bowery taverns and from the spire of Trinity Church, while Broadway, the *New York Herald* reported, "was almost hidden in a cloud of flaggery."[1]

Caught up in the spirit of the day, many men went straight from the rally and swamped recruiting stations to enlist in the army. They were confident that the war would be a short one and the Union would quickly be restored.

The Industrial North

There was good reason for their confidence. The nation had recently experienced a number of technological changes that had transformed many aspects of daily life. By fully utilizing these changes, the North had many significant material advantages over the enemy. These advantages would only increase as the North continually proved more adaptable to, and accepting of, even further changes.

Perhaps the most important change was increasing industrialization. While the country as a whole was still largely rural, the years before the war broke out saw an increasing number of factories being built. The vast majority of those were in the North. There were at least six times as many factories in the North as in the South, and the size of those enterprises is reflected in one simple statistic: for every Southerner who worked in a factory, there were twelve Northerners doing the same thing. In particular, the North had a virtual monopoly on shipbuilding and arms manufacturing. And the textile factories in the town of Lowell, Massachusetts, had more spindles spinning thread than the combined total of similar factories in the entire South. In addition, the North controlled most of the nation's coal, which provided the primary fuel for factories. As a result, in a matter of just a few years, the United States had become second only to England in worldwide manufacturing output.

Transportation and Communication

Another significant technological change was the explosive growth of railroads. Besides transporting people and supplies at previously unheard-of speeds, they were also a symbol of the weakening ties between the North and the South. Before the 1840s most railroad lines ran north and south. Then they switched directions, from west to east, and most of those new routes were in the North. As a result, the North had a distinct advantage, with more than 20,000 miles (32,187 km) of track (the South had less than half that total), plus much more rolling stock of better quality. Much of the cargo that Northern railroads carried was grain and other agricultural products from the fertile Midwest to help feed the increasing urban population, which was located primarily in the East.

> **WORDS IN CONTEXT**
> **rolling stock**
> Wheeled vehicles owned or used by a railroad company.

Union and Confederate States of the Civil War

Canada

WASH
TERR

OREGON

DAKOTA
TERRITORY

MINN

NEV
TERR

UTAH
TERR

NEBRASKA TERRITORY

COLORADO
TERRITORY

KANSAS

WIS

IOWA

MICH

ILL IND

MO

NH
VT   ME

NY

MASS

PA

RI
CONN
NJ
DEL
MD

OHIO

WV

VA

KY

NC

CALIF

NEW MEXICO
TERRITORY

INDIAN
TERR

ARK

TENN

SC

Territory

MISS ALA

GA

Confederate state

LA

TEXAS

FLA

Union state

0   400 mi

0   600 km

Mexico

When the war broke out, midwestern farms also helped provide food for the Union army. There was even enough to export to other countries. Farms became increasingly prosperous, which allowed their owners to afford newly introduced farm machinery. This machinery added to their yields and made them even more productive. In turn, relatively low-cost products manufactured in the East could be cheaply and easily transported to the farm states.

The telegraph, invented in 1844 by Samuel F.B. Morse, helped to coordinate this vast rail network. Tens of thousands of miles of telegraph lines—the vast majority in the North—had been erected and, in the process, had transformed communications. Newspaper publishers immediately embraced the new technology and for the first time were able to report on news stories as they occurred. They were aided by the patenting of the steam-powered rotary printing press in 1847 by Richard March Hoe. This press allowed newspapers to be printed far more quickly and cheaply than ever before.

As history professor Daniel W. Crofts notes, the result was that "mid-century Americans bought and read more newspapers than any other people on the face of the earth. The telegraph and newspapers combined to exert a uniquely powerful influence on American culture. No other part of the world was so affected."[2] The vast majority of newspapers were printed in the North, enabling people to stay in close touch with the events of the war as they unfolded.

The Northern Advantage

The Northern advantage even extended to the amount of money each side controlled. Historian Michael J. Varhola points out that "the Union controlled more than 80 percent of the total U.S. bank deposits, about $189 million, and about 60 percent of the total gold reserves, or about $56 million worth of gold. These factors immeasurably helped the North finance a successful war effort."[3]

The war effort lasted for almost four years, far longer than most people had expected. But those four years changed many of the ways that people lived their lives. Some of these changes were profound, while others were slight. Yet in some aspects, daily life in the North continued almost the same as it had been at the outbreak of the war.

Chapter One

Country Life

While there had been a trend in the years immediately preceding the Civil War toward moving into cities, most of the population in the North still lived on farms or in small towns. Despite increasing industrialization, agriculture remained by far the largest employer in the Union. Adding the transportation of food and the manufacturing and selling of farm equipment and supplies to actual farm labor, about three-fourths of Northerners made their living in some form of agriculture.

When the Civil War began, there were nearly 1 million farms in the North, with an average size of about 125 acres (51 hectares). In general, the farther west, the larger the average size—ranging from less than 100 acres (40 ha) in Rhode Island and Connecticut to more than 200 acres (81 ha) in states such as Illinois. New York, with more than 170,000 farms, had the largest number. It was trailed by Ohio, with more than 140,000, and Pennsylvania, which had nearly 130,000.

Increasing Prosperity

Farming had become increasingly prosperous in the years leading up to the Civil War. By the start of the war in 1861, many Northern farm families lived in relative comfort. They not only produced enough for their own needs but often had surpluses of crops or livestock that could be sold for a reasonable profit. Perhaps the key element in this prosperity was the use of machinery. As the *Cincinnati Gazette* noted in an article in November 1862, "we have reapers, mowers, separators, sowers, drills [etc.], making a great aggregate of agricultural machinery, which does the work of more

> **WORDS IN CONTEXT**
> **aggregate**
> Something formed by combining several different parts.

than three-fold the number of men, who (without machinery) would have been required to do it. . . . Besides, this machinery, which was at first only intended for large farms, now operates on the smallest."[4]

Things only improved for farmers as the war continued and the Union army expanded. All these troops needed to be fed, and the demand for farm produce grew accordingly. Notes Drew E. VandeCreek of Northern Illinois University:

> John Griffiths of Appanoose, Illinois epitomized farmers' high times during the Civil War. His son had gone to the army, receiving a bounty of $450 and wages of $25 a month. Much of this money went to expanding the farm. In the absence of laborers, John Griffiths completed most of the tasks himself. He built a new two-story house with a separate kitchen and cellar, and concluded that "It has been a good time for making money in the north since the war began. Everything was so high."[5]

Despite rapidly advancing industrialization in the North, much of the population still lived on farms or in small towns. A typical New England farm, as depicted by the well-known printmaker Currier & Ives, gives the appearance of prosperity even in the midst of winter.

Henry K. Dey, a farmer in New York, provided another example of the thriving Northern farm economy. In 1862 Dey sold his wheat for $1.00 a bushel. By the end of the war, he was getting nearly $2.50.

Historian Walter Gable points out that "as his income increased, he was increasingly making more trips to Geneva [the nearest town] to purchase what were becoming 'necessities of life'—rice, indigo, a tea steeper, whiskey, lemons, dry goods, coconuts, etc."[6]

Things Stay Almost the Same

Apart from receiving higher prices for their produce, in many ways the lives of Northern farmers remained virtually unchanged during the war. In a diary entry on January 25, 1862, New York farmer Isaac Hurlburt alluded to what was probably the January 19 Battle of Mill Springs when he wrote, "Got News of a battle in Kentucky."[7] Yet every other entry for the year records the seemingly timeless and mundane details of farm life: plowing, cutting wood, sowing, harvesting, riding in his sleigh, visiting friends, attending meetings, tapping trees for their syrup, the weather, and more. For example, on February 6, he referred to his twenty-one-year-old son when he wrote that "Edmond drew wood in the AM and Oiled the double Harness PM. I choped wood in the woods and Helped load when he drew. Had a pair of twin buck lambs come last night. Weather verry windy." On August 13 Hurlburt's entry stated, "Mowed the patch west of the Barn in AM. Boys drew in the last Hay on the Andrew lot two load and drew in one load wheat we mowed AM making three load. I cut the patch Oats north of the Barn."[8]

Even with the help of his sons, Hurlburt—like many other Northern farmers—needed a hired man to get everything done. So did Dey. Dey's "hired man worked from April 1 to December 1 for $75," notes Gable. "He was expected to do anything and everything on the farm: split wood, plow, harrow, help in harvest time, go to Geneva with goods to sell, pick stone, haul manure, and build fence. If he went fishing, to an auction or

In Their Own Words

Missing Their Men

Besides the physical toll that maintaining farms took on women whose husbands had gone off to war, there was considerable mental anguish. In a letter to her husband, Ben, in late 1863, Melissa Wells of Michigan doubtless expressed the feelings of countless numbers of other wives:

I have spent many gloomy and unhappy hours since you have been in the South. I hope I may never experience such feelings again for it is suffering indeed. Many times have I received a letter from you and would think that perhaps it was the last I would receive. . . . Many such times have I seen during the past two years, for instance when you relapsed and was sick with the fever at Murfreesboro. . . . I often think I never knew what trouble was until since the commencement of this horrid rebellion, but how many others there are who have learned the same by bitter experience.

Quoted in David Williams, *A People's History of the Civil War*. New York: New Press, 2005, p. 155.

something similar, he 'lost' the day, and Dey kept a careful record of his work."[9]

Women's Work

Life was not any easier for farm women. Their days often started even earlier than men's, when they rose to prepare a hearty breakfast so the men would have plenty of energy in the fields. As history professor Nicole

Etcheson observes, women also "cleaned the house, made clothes and laundered them, and helped with men's labor, especially during planting, butchering, and harvest times. . . . Historians agree that childbearing was among the most significant aspects of women's contribution to the farm. Children constituted the labor force."[10]

Like their husbands in the fields, farm wives often needed help. The solution was to hire girls—often from nearby farms—to help with the domestic workload. These girls typically earned around one dollar a week in addition to their room and board. Occasionally, they were allowed to return home briefly to visit their families.

Part of a Community

Many—if not most—individual farmers were self-sufficient during the Civil War, producing enough to take care of themselves. But few could survive without working together. "At harvest time, neighbors and their hired men came and aided in the work," Gable notes. "In the following weeks, the crops of each cooperating farmer were successively harvested. . . . Dey was dependent on his neighbors. He borrowed their machinery, traded or purchased cattle, and personally lived not alone but as part of a larger community."[11]

Fellow farmers were not the only source of support. A network of thousands of villages and small towns was essential to farmers' well-being. Ranging in size from a few hundred to a few thousand in population, these villages served as centers of commerce and community for the farms that surrounded them.

While some stores specialized in such necessities as feed for livestock and seeds for planting, the most important establishment was the general store. It stocked a variety of products such as roofing supplies, sugar and spices, salt and pepper, cigars and other tobacco products, oil, tea and coffee, dry goods, and much more. During the war, however, at least one item was in short supply in the North: sugar. The average person consumed more than 30 pounds (13.6 kg) of sugar annually on the eve of the war. With the customary supply line from the South suddenly shut down, the price of brown sugar and molasses more than doubled, and white sugar was almost unobtainable.

There was, however, no shortage of gossip. General stores also functioned as unofficial social centers, where farmers could check in with their friends and catch up on local news—especially news of loved ones away at war.

Getting the Latest News

General stores were not the only source of news. Virtually every small town produced a newspaper, typically containing four pages and appearing weekly or even more frequently. In an era long before television and the Internet, these newspapers were the primary source of

A vendor brings Philadelphia, New York, and Baltimore newspapers to the countryside in 1863. Newspapers, both small and large, carried news of the war and of happenings back home to people hungry for information.

information for people anxious about the progress of the war. As the Bowling Green State University (BGSU) library observes, "Because most [army] regiments were recruited in a specific locality, articles on the unit would appear in local newspapers, and servicemen's letters to the editor were often intended to represent the observations of the majority of the soldiers."[12]

It was not just the home folks who eagerly devoured each issue when it came out. For troops in the field, local newspapers were a way of staying in touch with their families and friends. Frequently, the men would pool their resources and take out a joint subscription to their hometown paper. Its arrival was always cause for rejoicing. As the BGSU library continues, "Certainly there was great interest in reports of combat and second-guessing of strategy, but there was also a continuing community narrative. Social relationships continued among the men and between the men and their families back home."[13]

School Days

Towns also were typically the site of the local school. Because few states offered public schools for everyone, churches or civic-minded citizens underwrote (guaranteed financial support for) the cost in many areas. There were very few official requirements for the contents of the curriculum or for hiring and firing teachers. They often had little more formal education than their students.

> **WORDS IN CONTEXT**
> **dry goods**
> Textiles, clothing, and related merchandise.

The war brought a number of changes to Northern education. Textbooks were rewritten to emphasize patriotism and the moral values of the North. ABC books for younger readers also changed. The word for O, for example, became "officer," while P was "president." Classroom recitals often included new songs and poems written specifically with the war in mind. In a journal entry dated May 20, 1861, Caroline Cowles Richards of Canandaigua, New York, wrote that "I recited 'Scott and the Veteran' to-day at school, and Mary Field recited, 'To Drum Beat and Heart Beat a Soldier Marches By.' . . . Every one learns war poems nowadays. There was a patriotic rally in Bemis Hall last night and a quartette sang, 'The Sword of Bunker Hill' and 'Dixie' and 'John Brown's Body Lies a Mouldering in the Grave,' and many other patriotic songs."[14]

Perhaps the most important change, though, came in the gender of the teachers. While increasing numbers of women had become teachers before the war, there was still a preference for men. Many of the male teachers departed for military service, however. Faced with the prospect of empty classrooms, many communities hired women to replace them. This was a financial advantage for communities, as female teachers were commonly paid less. And Cora Benton of Albion, New York, discovered a personal advantage. As historian David Williams notes:

> Pregnant with their second child when her husband went off to war, Cora at first hardly knew what to do. There were bills and taxes to be paid, children to feed, and not nearly enough income with which to do it. She finally decided to start her own boarding school and made it a great success. Before her husband returned, Cora felt so self-assured that she wrote to him, "There will be two heads after this do you understand darling?"[15]

Manpower Shortage

Single men from small towns and farms provided the majority of enlistees in the Union army. Their absence created a labor shortage that forced those who remained behind to work even harder. The hardships grew when married men left their families behind to join the fighting. Their wives had to take over the running of the farms, in addition to caring for children and their many customary household chores. In the beginning, at least, the work was especially exhausting. Barely able to move after a day in the fields she had spent hoeing potatoes, a farm wife in Michigan wrote to her husband, complaining of "lameness in my arms and a pair of hands pretty badly blistered. . . . It takes me a good while for I cannot work very fast."[16]

Not every wife approved of her husband's decision to enlist, especially since his absence could lead to economic hardship. "Now my dear husband let me tell you I do not verily believe I could live & bid you good bye to go in the Army how can you for a moment think of such a thing, can you leave me? can you leave our babes? no, no, no,"[17] wrote Alice Chapin of Indiana to her husband, Lucius, after he enlisted. In many cases husbands such as Lucius tried to control their households even though they were hundreds of miles away. Etcheson notes that "[Alice] found a position as a schoolteacher, but Lucius refused to give her permission to take it. He did not want 'a "School Ma'am" for a Wifey,' he wrote, so Alice gave up the idea, even reflecting that she might not have 'passed muster' anyway. She then tried to make money drying and canning produce."[18]

Many women poured out their feelings in letters to their relatives. Anna Schneider of Minnesota expressed the feelings of untold numbers of women:

> I am taking my pen in hand to tell you about the terrible situation I have to endure. I am writing and telling you that I am left alone with my four children in the woods because my husband has gone to War for one year. . . . I have to console myself that I am not alone without a husband. In my whole neighborhood there are only two men left. The rest are all gone and every woman has children.[19]

Women Take Up the Slack

Despite the difficulties, Northern farm women responded to the situation. As one soldier home on leave reported:

> The mother and the small brood carried on all the work of the farm as they were able. They cleared land, chopped down trees, and clad in brown denim dresses they burned the brush and cultivated the soil. They gathered and marketed the crops and thus became not only self-sustaining, but actually had a surplus with which to help the nation. Two girls, whom I well knew, became as expert in harvesting grain and in chopping wood as any man in the country.[20]

One thing that helped women was the increased availability of farm machinery. While they could not match their husbands in sheer strength, machinery allowed them to match or even exceed their previous output. This situation proved to be somewhat of a boon for farm equipment manufacturers, who quickly changed their advertising strategy. "Images within the ads showed women operating machines, demonstrating their

Looking Back

Patriotic Music in Northern Schools

Caroline Cowles Richards was typical of Union students in their attitude toward music. As Christian McWhirter of the National Archives observes:

> Northern schoolchildren were taught "Just before the Battle, Mother" and Henry Clay Work's "Washington and Lincoln." Student performances were often staged in dramatic fashion. In an Ohio school, children were drilled as a regiment and marched while singing patriotic songs. A St. Louis teacher had his students perform "The Battle Cry of Freedom" loud enough that "I hope the rebels hear us." Similarly, a Maryland teacher had her class sing this same song to passing Union troops. Other children hardly needed encouragement to play patriotic songs and behave like soldiers. One Michigan boy recalled that his friends frequently paraded around pretending to be military bandsmen, and newspapers reported high sales of fifes and drums designed for children.

Christian McWhirter, *Battle Hymns: The Power and Popularity of Music in the Civil War*. Chapel Hill: University of North Carolina Press, 2012, p. 103.

With the start of war, as men left to join the Union army, women took over many teaching positions. Some opened new schools in their communities. Others, such as this group of teachers, traveled to locations where their services were desperately needed.

ease of use for those women in charge of field work while men were off to the war," notes Iowa State University professor Robert C. Welch. "Other ads showed crippled veterans, most noticeably missing one arm, operating mowers or reapers. Those who returned maimed would still be able to farm due to modern technology."[21]

Women in the Fields

As the war drew on and more and more men joined the army, increasing numbers of women took to the fields. Mary A. Livermore, a journalist and philanthropist who devoted countless hours to the Union cause, toured several midwestern Union states in 1863 and wrote about her experiences in a book called *My Story of the War*. Pausing by one farm, she noted:

> Women were in the field everywhere, driving the reapers, binding and shocking, and loading grain, until then an un-usual sight. At first it displeased me, and I turned away in aversion. By-and-bye I observed how skilfully they drove the horses round and round the wheat field, diminishing more and more its periphery at every circuit, the glittering blades of the reaper cutting wide swathes with a rapid, clicking sound that was pleasant to hear. Then I saw, that where they followed the reapers, binding and shocking, although they did not keep up with the men, their work was done with more precision and nicety, and their sheaves had an artistic finish that those lacked made by men.[22]

At another farm, she talked to a woman, whose age she estimated at between forty-five and fifty, and her daughters. "I stepped over to where the girls were binding the fallen grain," Livermore wrote. "They were fine, well-built lassies, with the honest eyes and firm mouth of the mother, brown like her and clad in the same sensible costume."[23] One of the girls, named Annie, explained how she felt about working in the fields. "I tell mother . . . that as long as the country can't get along without grain, nor the army fight without food, we're serving the country just as much here in the harvest field as our boys are on the battlefield—and that sort o' takes the edge off from this business of doing men's work, you know."[24]

Struggling to Make Ends Meet

Livermore's almost idyllic descriptions did not apply to every farm headed by a woman whose husband was on the front lines. Despite their best efforts, some of these women simply could not make ends meet. In some cases family or friends helped them out. Theodore Upson, an Indiana farm boy, noted in a journal he began at the outbreak of the war that "we had another meeting at the school house last night; we are raising money to take care of the families of those who enlist. A good many gave money, others subscribed."[25]

More often, though, struggling farm women had nowhere to turn. To meet this need, a number of local aid societies sprang up, funded by donations from wealthy citizens in their respective communities. Many of these societies applied strict standards to potential recipients, who might be required to provide proof of their marriage to men on the front lines and swear that they were nearly destitute. Even then the money received was often a relative pittance. As Villanova University history professor Judith Giesberg notes, in late 1864 Maria Thomas of Pennsylvania "applied for relief from a local aid society, but she only received a few dollars to support herself and her children over the winter. When she wrote the governor in April 1865 she sought additional relief. 'My little Children is naked and I am very near naked.'"[26] The families of deserters had it even worse, because their support would often be cut off entirely even though the families were not at fault.

Patriotic Duty

Growing food for soldiers in the field came to be regarded as a patriotic duty. As New York's *Geneva Courier* proclaimed:

> Farmers—At this crisis in our country's history let not the farmer forget to make ample provisions for the thousands now rallying to hold up untarnished and cause forever to float that Star Spangled Banner—the pride of the world. . . . The farmers should double the amount of ground heretofore used for the various seeds and permit not a foot of soil to become account-less. . . . We entreat every farmer in the town(s) of Seneca and old Ontario to feel that they have an individual responsibility resting upon them.[27]

In general, farmers answered the *Courier*'s appeal. "President Lincoln's secretary of war. Edwin Stanton, credited the North's victory in the Civil War to farmers' keeping the soldiers supplied with bread," notes Giesberg. "Stanton was convinced that machines had made northern victory possible by releasing young men from the fields and insuring that the harvest was gathered though there were fewer hands to go around."[28] Of course, many of those "hands" belonged to women, who stepped up in a big way during the conflict and provided an uninterrupted flow of produce to the men on the front lines.

Chapter Two

City Life

Starting in late 1862 famed poet Walt Whitman spent nearly a year working as a nurse for wounded soldiers in Washington, DC. Exhausted by
his grueling regimen, and with several of his brothers and sisters needing
his help, Whitman took a train back to his hometown of Brooklyn, New
York. He passed through Baltimore and Philadelphia before getting off
at Manhattan. With memories of the horrors of the hospital still fresh in
his mind, Whitman found the trip to be a revelation. "It looks anything
else but war, everybody well dressed, plenty of money, markets boundless
& the best, factories all busy,"[29] he wrote.

By this time, nearly 6 million people lived in the increasingly indus-
trialized cities of the North. The five largest were New York City, with
815,000 people; Philadelphia, with a population of 570,000; Brooklyn,
with 270,000; Baltimore, with 215,000; and Boston, where 180,000
people lived.

Thriving Northern Cities

There was plenty of work. Northern shipyards built more than two hundred ships during the war and converted many existing vessels for war-
time use. Firearms factories such as Colt and Remington experienced
tremendous growth, often operating around the clock to produce rifles,
handguns, and cannons. Machines in the garment and shoemaking dis-
tricts clattered almost constantly, making uniforms and boots for the
fighting men.

Music was another growth industry. Many Union regiments had
their own bands, and the thousands of musicians needed instruments. In
addition, each company-sized unit was allotted a bugler and a drummer,

creating even more demand. One company produced more than sixty thousand trumpets and bugles during the war. And that was just the start. As Christian McWhirter of the National Archives points out, "The war's emotional, economic, and social impact on the nation encouraged the writing, production, distribution, and performance of music. . . . Only a year after the attack on Fort Sumter, the *Saturday Evening Post* observed that 'the National Music has aroused herself to meet the exigencies of the times.'"[30]

As many as ten thousand new patriotic songs and rewrites of existing ones that reflected the conditions of the conflict flooded the North in the form of sheet music. According to some estimates, music publishing became the most profitable form of print media. McWhirter cites one typical example involving Chicago-based publisher Root and Cady: "The firm printed more than 258,000 sheets of music and 100,000 music books in 1863 and in the fall of that year proudly announced that its songs could be heard even in Oregon. By the summer of 1864, high demand made it impossible to fill customer orders, and the firm had to purchase a second steam press."[31]

> **WORDS IN CONTEXT**
> **exigencies**
> Things that are required at a particular time or demand immediate attention.

Many Northern cities shared in this bounty. Chicago, en route to nearly tripling its population between 1860 and 1870, doubled its shipments of grain and meat within a year after the war started. The immense profits that were generated and the need to house the people who poured into the city led to a construction boom. In 1863 the *Chicago Tribune* reported, "On every street and avenue one sees new building going up: immense stone, brick, and iron business blocks, marble palaces and new residences everywhere."[32] These new structures led to additional jobs: grading streets, digging trenches for water pipes, building sewers, and more.

Change in the Capital

No Northern city underwent greater change than Washington, DC. When the war started, barely sixty thousand people lived there. Foreign

New York City, shown in a photograph taken during the Civil War, bustles with activity. Thriving factories and busy railroads ensured plentiful jobs and a continuous supply of items needed for daily living and for Union troops.

diplomats hated the city. It was hot and humid in the summer and cold in the winter, and it lacked many refinements of other Northern cities. As history professor David Goldfield notes, "Drainage ditches oozed with sewage and dead animals. Pigs rooted in the streets, and droves of cattle marched down thoroughfares as if the city were some displaced Kansas stockyard. . . . A startled visitor from Maine concluded that he had come to 'a squalid, unattractive, unsanitary country town infested by malaria, mosquitoes, cockroaches, bed bugs, lice, and outdoor backhouses."[33]

Washington had to grow up in a hurry. It became the nerve center of the nation as it undertook the almost infinite complications of moving from peace to war and managing that war. As the editors of *Civil War Washington* point out, "The Civil War fundamentally transformed Washington. The city changed physically, with prodigious construction of fortifications, government buildings, hospitals, transportation routes, residences, and new urban services."[34]

WORDS IN CONTEXT
backhouses
Outhouses, privies.

These new urban services were desperately needed. As television newsman and commentator Howard K. Smith noted, the city "could not adapt itself to the flash flood of humanity. The traffic of heavily laden army wagons and of troops with heavy equipment broke the backs of the thinly paved avenues, turning them into trenches of mud or channels of smoking dust."[35] Congress acted quickly, authorizing several private companies to construct streetcar lines in an effort to ease the problem. The first one opened in July 1862.

As *Civil War Washington* notes, part of the sudden swell in population consisted of "thousands of bureaucrats, actors, authors, doctors, nurses, and laborers . . . drawn to the capital by a sense of duty, opportunity, desperation, or adventure."[36] Because of Washington's proximity to the South, thousands of newly freed slaves also descended on the city. Still others were drawn by the increasing emphasis on science and invention in the capital. Lincoln was the only president ever granted a patent (for a device to lift boats over shallow water), and he took an active role in encouraging the development of scientific and technological innovations that would aid the Union cause. As a result of all these influxes, Washington's population had more than tripled by the end of the war.

Class Divisions

Not everyone shared equally in this war-induced prosperity. The social structure during the Civil War era resembled a pyramid: a small upper class with a great deal of money, a middle class, and the working class.

The wealthy upper class sought increasingly to separate themselves physically and socially from everyone else. They lived in large houses or mansions with large staffs of servants, while extensive gardens and vast, rolling lawns provided impressive settings for the stately homes. One primary aim of members of the upper class was to display their wealth, and homes often imitated European styles from the past.

Members of the upper class entertained themselves with a seemingly nonstop series of lavish gatherings such as masquerade balls. As Maria Lydig Daly, the wife of a New York judge, noted in early 1863:

> Last evening we went to Judge Bell's; the day before to a musical matinee at Mrs. James Brooks; Tuesday to a grand entertainment at Mr. Francis Cutting's on the occasion of his son's marriage. The beautiful bride and her eight pretty bridesmaids were very imposing with their long white veils. . . . The women dress as extravagantly as ever, and the supper and dinner parties are far more numerous than they have been for several winters.[37]

Middle Class

For most people, though, the pleasures of life were much simpler. For example, Walt Whitman and a friend named Peter Doyle "rode the streetcars together, drank at the Union Hotel bar, took long walks outside the city, and quoted poetry to each other (Whitman recited Shakespeare, Doyle limericks),"[38] according to Whitman scholars Ed Folsom and Kenneth M. Price.

Members of the middle class—people like Whitman and Doyle as well as merchants, shopkeepers, doctors, lawyers, and civil servants such as postal workers—tended to live in freestanding single homes or—more commonly—in row houses. These were two- or three-story structures built side by side, often sharing a common wall. The first floor contained the family rooms such as dining room, parlor, and kitchen, and bedrooms were upstairs.

Many wealthy Northerners lived in large houses surrounded by expansive lawns and gardens. One such estate is depicted in this Currier & Ives print from the period just before the start of the Civil War.

Working Class

The working class, which consisted primarily of factory workers and unskilled laborers, comprised at least 70 percent of the population in some cities. They commonly lived in tiny houses or "tenant buildings." These were two- to four-story wooden structures slapped together with little regard for safety. The rents were often exorbitant.

Living conditions in some tenant buildings challenged even the hardiest of working-class city dwellers. Lot sizes were regulated because of the grid layout of many cities—in New York, for example, they were 25 feet (7.6 m) wide by 100 feet (30.5 m) deep. So landlords sought to increase their rental income by erecting tenements. Made of flimsy materials that burned easily and constructed with minimal space between buildings, they were typically five or six stories in height. The average size of a single-room tenement apartment was about 300 square feet

(28 sq. m) or even less. Many did not have windows, and the circulation of fresh air was almost nonexistent. Although residents on the upper floors were required to take their trash down to the street where it could be disposed of in large garbage boxes, most simply dumped it down the air shaft. The shaft might be cleaned once a year, and the increasing piles of refuse created a horrible stench, in addition to providing an ideal environment for rats and other vermin. As the *New York Tribune* noted in 1863:

> **WORDS IN CONTEXT**
>
> **tenements**
>
> Flimsy buildings with tiny apartments having minimal sanitation and ventilation.

In front of each of these tenement blocks is placed a garbage-box, which is only another name for a receptacle of heterogeneous filth and corruption, composed of potato-peelings, cabbage-heads, turnips, dead lobsters, oyster-shells, night-soil, rancid butter, dead dogs and cats, and ordinary black street mud, all forming one breeding filth, reeking in the fierce sunshine which gloats yellowly over it like the glare of a devil whom Satan has kicked from his councils in virtuous disgust.[39]

In addition to often atrocious living conditions, many members of the working class faced another problem. Although their wages increased during the war, that increase was more than offset by an even greater increase in the prices of food and many other necessities. In 1863 the *Philadelphia Press* noted, "The war, which has stimulated business and trade, has reduced the value of money. . . . The increase in the price of many necessary articles of life, consume that portion of the laboring man's income that formerly went towards giving him some of the luxuries of life. Many a laboring man is fortunate if he can live at all."[40]

Life became even more difficult when the federal government began imposing taxes to finance the immense cost of the war. As historian James M. McPherson notes, "The Internal Revenue Act of 1862 taxed almost everything but the air northerners breathed."[41] Liquor, tobacco, playing cards, and medicine were just a few of the items that were taxed.

In Their Own Words

War? What War?

While poor people in Northern cities were often subjected to considerable hardships, the privation did not extend to members of the upper classes. They had money and the leisure time in which to enjoy spending it. As a *New York Herald* reporter of the time commented:

The kind of entertainment given seems to be of little account. Provided the prices are high and the place fashionable nothing more is required. . . . It is noticeable that the most costly accommodations, in both hotels and theatres, are the first and most eagerly taken. Our merchants report the same phenomenon in their stores: the richest silks, laces and jewelry are the soonest sold. . . . Not to keep a carriage, not to wear diamonds, not to be attired in a robe which cost a small fortune, is now equivalent to being a nobody. This war has entirely changed the American character. The lavish profusion in which the old Southern cotton aristocracy used to indulge is completely eclipsed by the dash, parade, and magnificence of the Northern shoddy aristocracy of this period. Ideas of cheapness and economy are thrown to the winds. The individual who makes the most money—no matter how—and spends the most money—no matter for what—is considered the greatest man.

Quoted in J. Matthew Gallman, ed., *The Civil War Chronicle*. New York: Gramercy, 2000, pp. 367–68.

As the war continued with no end in sight, workers became more and more angry with their economic situation. Many formed unions and—especially in 1863 and 1864—strikes became common. While some were successful, particularly in skilled trades, many others failed. One common reason for failure was the federal government. Baruch College history professor Edward Pessen notes:

> Military force was used against striking workers. Leaders in the strike at the famous Parrott gun works in Cold Springs, New York, were imprisoned without trial. In St. Louis, General Burbridge drove strikers back to work at the point of bayonets, while in St. Louis General Rosecrans charged picket lines and strike meetings. Soldiers in Tioga County, Pennsylvania, arrested the striking miners' leaders, forcing the rank and file to surrender to the owners under the threat of starvation.[42]

Women Flock to Factories

For tens of thousands of urban women, having their men off fighting the war was a financial catastrophe. In most cases their husbands' monthly army income was a fraction of what it had been from their jobs before the war, and even that relative pittance was often paid several months behind schedule. These women had little choice but to find work outside their homes. They poured into shops and factories, where they typically were paid less than men. Women and girls often worked eighteen-hour days sewing umbrellas for three dollars a week—minus the cost of needles and thread. Others earned two pennies an hour making shirts. Female workers at the US Army Arsenal in Allegheny, Pennsylvania, produced ammunition for fifty cents to a dollar a day. Women in Philadelphia's Schuylkill Arsenal—which employed thousands of seamstresses—received twelve cents for each backpack they produced. When some of them were fired they had to work for private contractors—who paid just a nickel for the same work.

WORDS IN CONTEXT
night-soil
Human excrement.

Coupled with rising prices, the low wages that women received created especially severe hardships. "We are unable to sustain life for the prices offered by contractors, who fatten on their contracts by grinding immense profits out of the labor of their operatives,"[43] a group of seamstresses wrote in 1864.

As depicted in this Civil War-era illustration of a munitions factory in Bridgeport, Connecticut, Northern women took over factory jobs once held by men. They worked long hours and received lower pay than their male counterparts but still thrived in these jobs.

Looking Back

A Tough Time to Be a Kid

Daily life was especially difficult for thousands of urban children. As historian David Williams notes:

> The war's impact on children was indeed heartrending. Hundreds of thousands were left fatherless, temporarily or permanently, in households that could not afford the lost income, little as it was. There was hardly any choice but for children to work or starve. They swept the street for what money passersby would throw their way. They sold newspapers, matches, and apples for what they could get. Some lived by gathering manure in the streets and selling it as fuel. Many found meager earnings at the textile mills, where in Massachusetts they made up 13 percent of the wartime labor force. In Pennsylvania's mills, their labor-force percentage was nearly one-fourth.
>
> Those were the fortunate ones. Many could find no work at all and wandered the streets as homeless beggars, sleeping in alleys and competing with dogs and each other in digging through trash piles for food. By 1863, there were as many as six thousand vagrant children in Boston. Estimates of those in New York City ranged as high as thirty thousand.

David Williams, *A People's History of the Civil War*. New York: New Press, 2005, p. 116.

And the working conditions could be hazardous. On September 17, 1862, a powerful explosion ripped through the Allegheny Arsenal. One young woman, Mary Jane Black, had left her work station a few minutes earlier to get her paycheck. It probably saved her life. As she told the coroner a few days later, she saw "two girls behind me; they were on fire; their faces were burning and blood running from them. I pulled the clothes off one of them; while I was doing this, the other one ran up and begged me to cover her."[44] Seventy-eight women and girls—some barely into their teens—perished.

Newspapers

Regardless of their social class, most people were avid newspaper readers. Oliver Wendell Holmes, a noted Boston physician and writer, summed up the value of newspapers in a letter to his son (a future Supreme Court justice) in 1861. "We must have something to eat, and the papers to read," he wrote. "Everything else we can do without. . . . Only bread and the newspaper we must have."[45]

The outbreak of the Civil War coincided with technological advances that made it possible to produce newspapers on a vastly increased scale while at the same time reducing their price to as low as a penny a copy and thereby broadening their circulation. Major cities such as New York and Philadelphia could boast of a dozen or even more dailies.

With war correspondents' stories coming in almost instantaneously on the telegraph wires, newspaper publishers kept the citizenry informed. Many papers supplemented such on-the-spot reports with lists of casualties, which readers scanned anxiously in search of news about the fate of their loved ones. In addition to straight reporting, newspapers often published political cartoons, which helped their readers understand some of the more controversial aspects of the war.

Crime Wave

Newspapers often carried accounts of a different kind of war: the war on crime. As the *New York World* noted in early January 1865:

The great increase in assaults with deadly weapons within the past year, as is shown by our police reports, is, of course, one of the penalties we are compelled to pay for being in a state of war. Men with military tastes get in the habit of carrying pistols and dirks [daggers], and, as a consequence, quarrels which otherwise have no worse result than a game of fisticuffs become homicides because of the handiness of deadly weapons.[46]

Men with guns were not the only reason for the increase in the crime rate. Many people, especially women and children whose husbands or fathers were off at war, faced a choice between starving and stealing food. Of course, theft always carried the risk of being caught. By 1863 the population of the House of Refuge, a New York City children's prison, had increased by 68 percent. At the end of the war, even that elevated number had nearly doubled. One Massachusetts prison official of the time, commenting on the link between the war and juvenile crime, remarked, "I have talked with many boys in Jails and Houses of Correction who were either sons or brothers of soldiers or sailors in the service."[47] Girls were as just as susceptible. George Templeton Strong, a New York lawyer, noted in his diary that "no one can walk the length of Broadway without meeting some hideous troop of ragged girls, from twelve years old down, brutalized already almost beyond redemption . . . with thief written on their cunning eyes."[48]

Women, too, packed the jails in ever-increasing numbers. The number of female inmates in Massachusetts county jails tripled during the war. New York's Sing Sing Prison doubled its female population. By the end of the war, nearly half the inmates in Detroit's House of Correction were women.

This situation was the dark side of Walt Whitman's observation about the prosperity in the cities he passed through. While factories were indeed very busy and many people well-dressed, others struggled just to stay alive.

Chapter Three

Building and Sustaining an Army

At the outbreak of the Civil War, the US Army numbered about sixteen thousand officers and men. Apart from a few skirmishes with Indians as settlers pushed westward, the army had not been in any significant engagements since the end of the Mexican-American War in 1848. Nor did it inspire respect from other Americans. As historian Adam Goodheart notes, "The peacetime 'regular army' . . . was considered a last resort for men who couldn't get by otherwise in the merciless economy of nineteenth-century America—or the first resort of immigrants with no resources or connections."[49]

That attitude changed almost literally overnight when Confederate cannons fired on Fort Sumter. Even though no Union troops were killed in the bombardment, Northerners—many of whom had never heard of Fort Sumter—viewed its surrender as a national disgrace. They wanted vengeance. Though Lincoln was not motivated by vengeance, he struggled mightily to preserve the Union. For that he needed a lot of men—and he needed them right away. He immediately issued a call for seventy-five thousand troops.

Answering Lincoln's Call

Fired by a patriotic zeal, men by the tens of thousands flocked to sign up. While there were wide variations in age and occupation, the typical Union soldier was young, single, white, Protestant, and from a rural background. Officers usually came from the middle and upper classes. Whatever their rank, the men had a variety of reasons for enlisting.

Though a few abolitionists said that they wanted to help free the slaves, Henry W. Tisdale of Massachusetts—who was a twenty-five-year-old clerk in a trading business when he enlisted—spoke for the vast majority of his new comrades when he wrote in his diary: "I felt it my duty to be one of them [soldiers], feel it as much a Christian as a political duty, and feel that every citizen ought to feel it so. And certainly have never felt more peace of mind as flowing from a sense of duty done, as in this matter of enlistment into the service of our country."[50]

Ulysses S. Grant, a one-time army officer who had graduated from the US Military Academy at West Point and was having difficulty adjusting to civilian life, wrote at the outbreak of the war to his father:

Evry one must be for or against his country, and show his colors too, by his every act. Having been educated for such an emergency, at the expense of the Government, I feel that it has upon me superior claims, such claims as no ordinary motives of self-interest can surmount. . . . I have but one sentiment now. That is we have a government, and laws and a flag and they must all be sustained. There are but two parties now, Traitors & Patriots, and I want hereafter to be ranked with the latter.[51]

Grant would eventually lead the Union army to victory and later be elected as president.

Other men joined for practical reasons. One of these men was Lucius Chapin of Indiana, who had found little success in the working world and badly needed income to support his family, including a sick wife. History professor Nicole Etcheson observes:

Years later [after the war] Lucius Chapin would recall that he had enlisted in early 1862 out of patriotism, but at the time he emphasized the economic benefits to his family. . . . Chapin had tried a number of occupations by the early 1860s and made a successful living at none of them. Alice's ill health, probably stemming from pregnancy and childbirth, had left them with large medical bills. . . . Lucius used the Army to make a new start.[52]

In theory every volunteer had to submit to a physical examination to demonstrate fitness for the rigors of warfare. Many of these examinations were cursory at best. Historians have documented at least 250 women on both sides who managed to elude detection of their sex and join the conflict. According to the Library of Congress's Teaching with Primary Sources website, "Like male soldiers, women were motivated by a variety of factors. In addition to the thirst for adventure and the desire to accompany loved ones [husbands, fiancés and male relatives], women served out of dedication to a cause and out of a need to earn money for their families. Most female soldiers remained undetected as women unless they were wounded or killed."[53]

Most regiments were assembled with men from a single state and were numbered in the order in which they were established. As historian Geoffrey Ward points out, "Whole towns signed up. The 10th Michigan Volunteers was comprised entirely of Flint men; their commander was the mayor; their regimental doctor had been caring for them since they were boys."[54] Most regiments consisted of ten companies, which included between 83 and 101 men. In the beginning, each company elected its own officers. Typically, recruits joined newly established regiments, rather than serving as replacements for regiments depleted by battle casualties or disease. During the course of the war, the North raised more than 2,000 regiments: nearly 1,700 infantry, 272 cavalry, and 78 artillery.

The Draft

Despite early battlefield setbacks, Northern enthusiasm for the war remained high, and by early 1862 Secretary of War Edwin Stanton called for a slowdown in enlistments. But later that year, as the war dragged on with no end in sight and word of its horrors spread, Lincoln issued a call for a further three hundred thousand troops for three-year stints. When that number proved to be insufficient, Lincoln requested yet another three hundred thousand men for nine-month enlistments. If states did not meet their federally mandated enlistment quotas, they had to conduct a draft using a lottery system to raise enough men.

The draft was highly unpopular and often resulted in rioting. In Port Washington, Wisconsin, a mob of angry farmers—many of them German immigrants, who had no desire to become part of what they believed was a war sponsored by abolitionists—attacked William A. Pors, an attorney acting as draft commissioner, as he began to conduct the lottery in November 1862. After beating him nearly unconscious, the rioters burned the records of the men who were eligible and clomped

Posters seek recruits for the Union army in New York in 1864. When the draft failed to bring in the needed numbers, towns began offering bounties of several hundred dollars in hopes of attracting new recruits.

off to ransack his house. According to a newspaper account of the time, "The furniture was smashed up and dumped into the street. Jellies, jams, and preserves were poured over the Brussels carpet, and ladies' apparel torn into shreds."[55] The mob attacked other businesses and homes and injured dozens of people. Governor Edward Salomon dispatched several hundred troops, who quickly restored order and arrested more than one hundred men. Pors returned a few days later and finished the lottery. In spite of the damage to his house, Pors was more fortunate than some other draft officials, who were killed as they tried to perform their duties.

Another reason for the violent opposition to the draft was that it favored the well-to-do. If their names were drawn, they could hire someone to take their place, or they could pay a $300 fee in lieu of serving. Those who could afford it could also pay

> **WORDS IN CONTEXT**
> **mandated**
> Required, ordered.

doctors to write up bogus medical conditions that would exempt them from service. In 1863 the *New York Illustrated News* somewhat sarcastically noted that "the prospect of involuntary service develops an amount of latent diseases and physical disabilities that are perfectly surprising."[56]

Bounties Offered

Where the draft failed to deliver the needed numbers, the bounty system helped to take up the slack. It was yet another means of getting men to enlist. As Tisdale observed, "All towns are offering liberal bounties, varying from one to three hundred dollars. I fear that some of our volunteers go more from motives founded in dollars and cents than from those drawn from true patriotism."[57]

Tisdale's concern was fully justified. Such men often proved to be terrible soldiers. The bounty system also led to the rise of bounty jumpers. These were men who would sign up, collect their bounty, and desert at the first opportunity. They would travel to another region, sign up again under a different name, and collect another bounty—twenty or more times in extreme cases. The Springfield, Massachusetts, newspaper the *Republican* sniffed at this practice:

Two scamps named James Hayden and Francis Leonard, Englishmen by birth, who were previously employed at the factories in Indian Orchard, were arrested as deserters in this city by Officer Shaw. They have enlisted under various aliases in this state and Connecticut and after getting the bounty deserted. . . . This getting the bounty from the government and then deserting, is the meanest of all mean things. But what better could we expect from Englishmen.[58]

Drills and More Drills

In the aftermath of the disastrous Battle of Bull Run in July 1861, General George McClellan took command of Union forces. Realizing that the war was likely to last much longer than most people had believed before the battle, McClellan imposed a stringent series of new rules. Hardly any of his men had had any military experience before the battle. Typical was nineteen-year-old Elisha Hunt Rhodes, a Rhode Island harness maker's clerk, who enlisted as a private. He began keeping a diary of his experiences and noted that after one day, "I was elected First Sergeant, much to my surprise. Just what a First Sergeant's duties might be, I had no idea."[59]

Leading an army that consisted primarily of men like Rhodes, McClellan knew they needed to become much more disciplined. The chief method of achieving this goal was a rigorous schedule of drills. These drills began with small units, then expanded to include regiments and even larger groups. As Pennsylvania private Oliver W. Norton observed, "The first thing in the morning is drill, then drill, then drill again, then drill, drill, a little more drill, then drill, and lastly drill. Between drills we drill and sometimes stop to eat a little and have a roll call."[60]

While Norton doubtless exaggerated, McClellan wanted his men to stay occupied. In addition to the seemingly endless drilling, they were responsible for keeping their living quarters neat and tidy, making sure

In Their Own Words

Why Men Fought and Died

In a letter to his hometown newspaper at the beginning of 1864, Baron Crane of the Twenty-Fifth Iowa Infantry reflected on the men in his unit who had been killed.

When I see our short line on parade and think of the time when our Colonel's voice would hardly reach from one end to the other, I am compelled to think of the dark side of the picture. Many, very many of those whose faces seem before me now, have fallen, martyrs to the sacred cause of liberty. Their bodies lie for a thousand miles along Mississippi's turbid water and amid the dark Cypress swamps of Louisiana and Mississippi, and Lookout's lofty peak looks down upon them gently reposing among the hills and valleys of Tennessee and Alabama. They died far away from home, with no loving hand to smooth their dying pillows, yet many of them gave up their lives feeling "that it was sweet for one's country to die." Their lives have not been spent in vain. Their memory will live with us and incite us to nobler deeds of daring, and in after days we will speak their names softly to our children and tell them to emulate them in their devotion to their country. . . . We have no idea of quitting the contest until every foot of territory belonging to the United States be reclaimed, and the last traitor ceases to lift his hand against this great and good Government.

Quoted in Ann Crane Salzman Farriar, ed., *Baron Hutchinson Crane: His Civil War Letters.* Parma, OH: privately printed, 2000, p. 17.

their equipment was well maintained, gathering firewood and water, building roads, digging trenches and latrines, and everything else needed to keep their camps functioning like small cities.

Discipline

Discipline was harsh and unremitting. Any one of the hundreds of possible offenses—including falling asleep on guard duty, drunkenness, defying orders, and rowdiness—could lead to punishments that were physically painful and designed for maximum humiliation. Men might be compelled to wear a "barrel shirt"—a barrel with holes cut in the sides and top for the arms and head to protrude. Or an offender might have to parade through the camp bearing a log on his shoulders. For petty crimes such as theft, a man might have his head shaved and be "serenaded" through the camp with a fife and drum while wearing a placard spelling out his offense. Even worse was "bucking and gagging." According to one New Jersey soldier who apparently witnessed this punishment, "A bayonet or piece of wood was placed in his mouth and a string tied behind his ears kept it in position, then the man was seated on the ground with his knees drawn up to his body. A piece of wood is run through his legs, and placing his arms under the stick on each side of his knees, his hands are then tied in front, and he is as secure as a trapped rat."[61]

Some punishments lasted far more than a single day. As Jerry Flint of the Wisconsin Fourth Infantry/Cavalry noted in a letter on September 14, 1861, to his brother, "A man in our regiment attempted to strike his Lieut. His sentence is solitary confinement for 30 days, besides forfeiting one half his pay for six months. In Baltimore a man was found drunk while on guard. He had to walk a ring under charge of the guard for 30 days carrying a knapsack weighing 20 lbs."[62]

Camps

These punishments were deemed necessary to regulate the behavior of thousands of men over extended periods of time, especially while they were in camps. Such camps often included several regiments totaling five thousand men or even more. While the army was on the march, the

Soldiers in the Union army sometimes lived in primitive log cabins or, as in this 1864 photograph of members of the 6th Army Corps, in tents. The lucky ones slept on mattresses stuffed with straw, pine needles, or leaves.

troops were sheltered in tents that held up to twenty men. Flies, mosquitoes, ants, and bedbugs were a constant source of irritation. So was the smell. David Lane of the Seventeenth Michigan Volunteer Infantry said, "That which troubles and annoys me most, others do not seem to mind. It is the intolerable, nauseating stench that envelops a military camp. My olfactories have become so acutely sensitive I can smell an encampment 'afar off.'"[63] To try to combat the stench and maintain some level of hygiene, the men washed their clothes whenever they had the opportunity. If they camped near a stream or river, many would plunge in and wash away the accumulated grime of endless miles of marching.

The campaigning season typically lasted until late November or early December, when rain and snow made roads impassable. Then the men would establish more durable camps and wait until the weather improved and roads finally dried out the following spring. The primary advantage of these winter camps was the ability to construct primitive log cabins, filling the gaps between the logs with mud and wood chips to keep out

Looking Back

Off to War

With most Northerners eager to punish the South for its effrontery—and fully believing that administering the punishment would not take very long—Lincoln's call for volunteers inspired a spirited response. New York City officials guaranteed that the city by itself would provide two-thirds of the men Lincoln asked for. As historian Adam Goodheart notes:

> "All the world wants to march," wrote one of Lincoln's confidants. In New York, the first soldiers to depart for Washington were members of the high-society Seventh Regiment, who sashayed down Broadway in their fine gray uniforms, with heavy dirks and bowie knives tucked into each felt for hand-to-hand fighting, and cigars in each hatband for the more leisurely hours of soldiering. (At least a few fashion-conscious militiamen, it was said, had stashed white kid gloves in their knapsacks, thoughtfully preparing to dress appropriately for the victory balls in Washington in just a few weeks' time). . . . In a small town in Maine, thirty-odd veterans of the War of 1812 proclaimed themselves a military company and pledged to totter off southward into the thick of the fighting. . . . An Indian chief named Pug-o-na-ke-shick, or Hole-in-the-Day, an ex-major of the Ottoman [Turkish] Army, as well as several bellicose groups of Canadians, all offered their services.

Adam Goodheart, *1861: The Civil War Awakening*. New York: Vintage, 2012, pp. 209–10.

the chill winds. Roofs were made of boards, shingles, or even part of the tents. For heat, the men made fireplaces or used stoves. Besides bunks with primitive mattresses filled with straw, pine needles, or leaves, they furnished their quarters with ammunition crates for tables and sat on stumps or packing cases. To keep their feet dry when they ventured outside, they built wooden walkways. Some of the structures were substantial, housing well over one hundred men.

The Importance of Food

No matter what the season, food was always a priority. For recruits from farming areas accustomed to tasty and nutritious fresh meals, army food was a severe shock. Because of the lack of refrigeration, meat—primarily pork and beef—was heavily salted to preserve it and thus needed to be soaked in freshwater to make it even remotely palatable. Fresh fruits and vegetables were a rarity.

The mainstay of the diet was hardtack. Consisting of a mixture of flour, water, and salt, it was baked in 3-inch (7.6 cm) squares. As the name suggested, it was extremely hard, and because it had to be softened in water before eating, it acquired grim nicknames such as "teeth dullers." It was not hard enough, though, to prevent weevils from burrowing inside. According to historian William C. Davis, "A New England soldier advised that the crackers be soaked in coffee first—some said six weeks was long enough—and then laid on a plate, taking care not to shake the worms out. 'They eat better than they look,' he said, 'and are so much clear gain in the way of fresh meat.'"[64]

> **WORDS IN CONTEXT**
> **olfactories**
> Relating to the sense of smell.

The men loved coffee, especially during cold weather. It also helped to keep them awake during the long periods of inactivity. The men would be provided with raw green coffee beans, which they would roast over an open fire in a skillet. Then they would crush the beans, frequently using the butts of their rifles, and boil the grounds. It was a particular treat after long marches. Men would drink cup after cup and still have no trouble falling asleep.

Union soldiers did not hesitate to scrounge better meals as they marched through Confederate territory. In a letter on December 8, 1862, from his encampment near Holly Springs, Mississippi, Charles Wright Wills of the Eighth Illinois Infantry wrote, "My company 'found' 150 pounds of flour, a hog, a beef, two and one-half bushels of sweet potatoes, chickens, ducks, milk, honey and apples. The night we stopped at Holly Springs, Company G must have confiscated $300 (the way these people figure) worth of eatables, among which were one barrel of molasses, 300 pounds of sugar, one barrel of flour, four hogs, etc."[65]

Baron Crane of the Twenty-Fifth Iowa Infantry enjoyed a welcome addition to his rations in late August 1864 as his unit was about to enter Atlanta, Georgia. "Green corn is large enough to eat and we are getting a plenty of it & living finely," he wrote. "Our cook has got to grating the corn off the cob and making mush and we have a cow which gives plenty of milk so we are having that great luxury mush and milk tho I never before thought it a luxury."[66]

Officers enjoyed better living conditions than enlisted men. Shortly after capturing a small Southern town, Lieutenant Josiah Marshall Favill of the Fifty-Seventh New York Infantry noted one of the perks of being an officer: "As most of the best houses were deserted when we arrived, the officers found no difficulty in securing good quarters. The difference between a good house, even if it is empty, and an ordinary shelter tent, late in November, is immense, and the officers fully appreciate it."[67] Lieutenants received a base pay about eight times that of privates, and higher ranks made even more. Many officers also employed servants—usually blacks—to prepare food for them and provide other services. In a letter to his brother on July 25, 1864, on the outskirts of Atlanta, Crane noted that he "hired a nigger servant yesterday to wait on me take care of my horse."[68]

Animal Mascots

With reminders of death and destruction a constant presence, men sought comfort in any way they could. One primary source of such comfort was pets, who often served as mascots. Dogs were by far the most common, though other pets included cats, squirrels, raccoons, badgers, pigeons, and even a couple of bears. The Ninth Connecticut Infantry had a trained pig named Jeff Davis, after the Confederate president. In many cases the animals came from the regiments' hometowns and provided a connection with the life the men had left behind. In other instances they were strays who wandered into camp and were quickly adopted.

Being a regimental mascot could be dangerous. Jack, a dog who belonged to the 102nd Pennsylvania Infantry, was captured in May 1863 with a number of members of the regiment and spent six months in Richmond's Libby Prison before being released. Some dogs were killed during battles and buried along with men from their regiments.

The most famous mascot was Old Abe the War Eagle. Named for the president, the bird was the mascot of the Eighth Wisconsin. He perched on a shield-shaped stand with a tether that allowed him to fly a few feet away and reportedly accompanied his regiment to thirty-six battles without ever losing a feather. As the regiment's sergeant major George Driggs explained

Cooks in the Union's 2nd Rhode Island Infantry regiment take a break from their work in the camp kitchen. Army food consisted mainly of hardtack—an unappetizing mixture of flour, salt, and water—and heavily salted and preserved meats.

in a memoir he published in 1864, "The regiment has become so attached to him, by his long habitation with us, that, rather than lose him, or see him fall into the hands of the enemy, every man would spend his last cartridge in his defence. [Confederate] General [Sterling] Price has been said to declare that he would rather 'capture that bird than a whole brigade.'"[69]

Finding Comfort in Prayer

Attending church services also comforted the soldiers. Many troops were very devout and relished the opportunity to observe the Sabbath. As George Grenville Benedict of the Twelfth Vermont Volunteers noted in a letter to his hometown newspaper in Burlington in November 1862:

> Many as are the contrasts between our life in the army and that we lead at home, there is none greater than that between our Sabbaths there and here. As we stood at regimental service yesterday, our chapel a vacant spot before the colonel's tent, our heads canopied only by the grey clouds drifting swiftly to the southwest, and the chill November wind blowing through our ranks, I could not but cast back a thought to the quiet and comfortable New England sanctuaries many of us have been wont to worship in. But we were better off than most of the regiments in the army, for but few of them, probably, had any Sabbath service at all.[70]

Sometimes religious observances extended beyond the Sabbath. On the eve of the Battle of Antietam in 1862, a brigade composed almost entirely of Irish immigrants was placed in one of the riskiest positions on the battlefield. History professor Terry L. Jones of the University of Louisiana at Monroe notes, "Father William Corby, one of the brigade's chaplains and future president of [the University of] Notre Dame, rode down the firing line and administered a general rite of absolution to the men."[71]

Especially on the eve of battle, men prayed that they would survive and welcomed the intercession of chaplains such as Corby. But they were fully aware of the grim mathematics of war. They knew that many of them would not survive.

Chapter Four

Taking Care of the Troops

From the beginning of the Civil War, supporting the troops became an important aspect of daily life for many people in the North. This support took a number of forms, which included providing moral and material support to the men in the field, taking care of the wounded and ill, and providing physical and financial assistance.

Keeping in Touch

Few things meant more to soldiers in the field than staying in touch with their families and loved ones through the mail—and in some cases with girls they did not know and almost certainly would never meet but who felt it their patriotic duty to correspond with soldiers. Andrew F. Sperry of the Thirty-Third Iowa Infantry spoke for soldiers everywhere when he wrote about the arrival of a supply train: "The greatest joy was over the 'good old mail' which came with the train. . . . Little could the writers of those letters imagine, how eagerly the envelopes were torn open, or how dear and precious the words of love and hope, seemed to us, there in the enemy's country."[12]

The arrival of mail, no matter what time of day or night, was always a cause for rejoicing. In August 1863 Baron Crane wrote to his brother:

Just a few moments ago I was lying in my bunk, winking and trying to go to sleep and pass away a portion of the weary time, when the cry of "Fall in for your mail" roused me up in an instant and I was soon mingling with the eager crowd for my share of home news. Nor was I disappointed. I got three letters & three papers and have been enjoying myself hugely while perusing them. As your faces seem before me, fresh as ever & my feelings and affections burn within, toward, home, I don't see how I can pass a more pleasant hour than to pen a reply to your inquiries after my welfare.[73]

The volume of mail was staggering, with hundreds of millions of letters going back and forth. While most letters to soldiers were written in ink, the return correspondence was often in pencil. A pencil or two was much easier to carry than fragile pens and bottles of ink. A broken ink bottle not only meant lost ink for writing but likely stained clothing too. Letter writing came with other challenges as well. Finding a firm writing surface could be difficult, especially for enlisted men, and many letters were composed on the head of a drum that served as a table.

The relatively new field of photography provided another way of maintaining close bonds. Recent technical advances such as the tintype photograph were affordable and could be produced in a matter of minutes. Many towns had photo studios. If not, families might use traveling photographers who could produce an image in a few minutes in their portable darkrooms. Before leaving for the war, many men took family pictures to remind them of what they had left behind. Some photographers visited encampments so soldiers could provide their loved ones with current images.

Clothing

Many families sent packages, which might contain food but often included clothing such as shirts, pants, and mittens. Some of the most welcome parcels contained underwear, which consisted of a baggy undershirt that dangled below the wearer's waist and drawers that were at least knee length and often extended to the ankles. Many men preferred waiting to receive new underwear rather than carrying extra pairs to change into. Packing extra sets added still more weight to their already heavy packs.

Keeping underwear and other clothing clean presented problems for troops on the march. Washing was a difficult, time-consuming process,

More than anything else, troops looked forward to receiving letters from home. They also sent letters to family whenever time permitted. Women, frequently nurses, helped injured soldiers with their letter-writing, as depicted in this sketch from 1863.

In Their Own Words

Delivering the Mail

Each regiment had a postmaster, whose sole responsibility was the distribution of mail. It was not a coveted position. As Private William Morrow of the Sixty-Third Pennsylvania Regiment observes, the postmaster

was excused from other duties, such as drill, guard mount, etc., but that was small recompense for the annoyance he had to endure. People are the same the world over, and all deem it a privilege to growl and swear at the postmaster. It mattered not how cold, or wet, or hot, or disagreeable it might be, the regimental postmaster must always be on time; if he was late the officers would give him a blowing up and the men would abuse him. When he arrived in camp with his mail sack, he was an object of interest to all. Those who received letters were satisfied for the time, and those who did not get any, apparently seemed to think it was his fault and expressed their opinion of him in a manner that was not at all complimentary. Once our mail carrier fell in a creek and lost his sack, and how he was cursed and abused. We all felt certain that the lost sack contained letters for each one of us, and if the carrier had been drowned and the mail matter saved, we would have been much better satisfied.

Quoted in Gilbert Adams Hays, ed., *Under the Red Patch: Story of the Sixty Third Regiment; Pennsylvania Volunteers, 1861–1864*. Pittsburgh, PA: Market Review, 1908, p. 146. http://archive.org.

and many men balked at this work. To solve the problem, four laundresses were allocated to each company. Many were married to someone in the company they served and typically had at least a child or two to care for. They were paid directly by the men. A typical rate was fifty cents per month for enlisted men, while officers—who usually had more clothing—paid a higher rate. Because they were officially recognized by the army—which required them to have a Certificate of Good Character—laundresses received a ration of food, wood for fuel (though they had chop it themselves), primitive accommodations, and transportation when the company was on the move.

Laundry day began with getting water. It had to be hauled from a nearby source such as a creek in heavy oak tubs that weighed more than 30 pounds (13.6 kg) when empty. In winter the laundress might have to chop up ice to melt for wash water. While waiting for the water to warm, she sorted the clothing into piles by color and fabric. Detergent was prepared beforehand by dissolving soap shavings in hot water to make a kind of paste, which was then stirred along with the clothes in the pots. Eventually, the clothes were removed and rinsed two or even three times—with every piece firmly wrung by hand after each rinse. Then the clothing was hung up to dry. Often there were rips and tears to be mended or buttons to replace. Finally—often several days later—the men had their clothes back, grateful that someone else had done all the work.

> **WORDS IN CONTEXT**
> **sutler**
> A civilian who followed the army, selling food and other provisions to the soldiers.

Civil War Convenience Stores

Another important element in maintaining morale was the sutler system. While the army provided basic necessities, often the men wanted more and better food, clothing, reading material, tobacco, and so on. Sutlers accompanied the soldiers in the field—in effect acting as mini general stores.

Although sutlers were civilians, they were licensed by the army. Each regiment was allowed one sutler, who was supposed to sell items of decent quality at reasonable prices. In practice, however, their food

Soldiers who could afford it often purchased additional food, clothing, and other items from licensed vendors known as sutlers. One group of sutlers appears in this photograph from around 1862. Sutlers were supposed to sell decent-quality items at reasonable prices, but this was rarely the case.

often was spoiled, while their clothing might last for just a few weeks. And many charged exorbitant prices, such as sixty cents for a dozen eggs and even more for a pound of butter—a hefty chunk from a private's meager earnings. Sutler's pies were more reasonably priced at twenty-five cents, though according to a popular saying, they were "moist and indigestible below, tough and indestructible above, with untold horrors within."[74]

Still, there was no denying the appeal of the provisions offered by sutlers. When he arrived at his campsite near the Virginia town of Aquia Springs in 1862, Captain George F. Noyes of New York suffered a moment of dismay before he realized that the camp had a sutler's tent:

The little collection of rough-board shanties and tents, thrown up in a day, crowded with soldiers, and clamorous with the usual bustle of the quarter-master's department, offered so few gastronomic advantages that we were just about to despair, when a current of blue uniforms, every man with a handful of pie and cheese, indicated a sutler's tent. Entering by the rear, we were soon sitting round a barrel-head table, feasting on coffee, cakes, and cheese with infinite gusto and merriment.[75]

Caring for the Wounded

No matter the level of morale, every man was grimly aware that he could be wounded or killed. Because there were just over one hundred doctors in the Union army when the Civil War began, they were quickly overwhelmed. Eventually, the army would employ more than twelve thousand physicians, many of them with little medical experience—and virtually none of it in dealing with battlefield wounds. Improvements in military technology had vastly increased the range and destructive power of weapons, making doctors' jobs much more difficult. Perhaps the most widespread of these weapons was the minie ball, which has been called the first modern bullet. Because they expanded when they struck their targets, they created gaping wounds. Men shot in the head, chest, or abdomen had virtually no hope of survival. Even those shot in the arms or legs were in peril. The force of the bullet shattered bones and drove dirt and clothing deep into the wound, increasing the likelihood of infection or gangrene.

In many such cases the wounded man's only hope for survival was the immediate amputation of the injured limb. According to one witness:

Tables about breast high had been erected upon which the screaming victims were having legs and arms cut off. The surgeons and their assistants, stripped to the waist and bespattered with blood, stood around, some holding the poor fellows while others, armed with long, bloody knives and saws, cut and sawed away with frightful rapidity, throwing the mangled limbs on a pile nearby as soon as removed.[76]

Experienced surgeons could perform amputations in ten to fifteen minutes. The severed limbs would be tossed onto ever-growing piles that were eventually buried.

Mild anesthetics such as chloroform and ether reduced some of the suffering of men who were undergoing amputation. On the other hand, doctors had not learned of the role of cleanliness in preventing infection. As history professor Terry L. Jones notes:

> The Civil War may have been a fight of brother against brother, but it was equally a fight of brother against microbe. The Union Surgeon General, William A. Hammond, famously claimed the Civil War "was fought at the end of the medical Middle Ages." In 1864, Louis Pasteur had discovered that germs caused diseases, but his breakthrough was not widely accepted at the time, and Joseph Lister did not publish his findings on the use of antiseptics until two years after the Civil War ended.[77]

Surgeons operated while wearing gowns soaked with blood and pus. With hundreds of men waiting for treatment, they did not have the time (or the knowledge) to thoroughly clean themselves after every operation. They commonly used the same instruments over and over without cleaning them.

Disease Even More Deadly

The horrors of battlefield hospitals were bad enough. Yet they were not even the deadliest aspect of the war. In the field, each day began with a regimental "surgeon's call." There was rarely a shortage of responses. Some men had sustained injuries in camp. Alfred Bellard, writing during the Chancellorsville, Virginia campaign, which lasted from April 30 to May 6, 1863, explains one such injury:

> One drummer boy was brought in to be operated upon, who had both hands shattered by the explosion of a gun barrel. He had picked up a gun barrel on the field, and was holding it in

the fire to have a little fun, when it exploded. His hands were shattered all to pieces, saving nothing but a thumb on one hand, and a thumb and finger on the other. When the doctors had him on the table and under the influence of cloraform [chloroform], they picked out the pieces of bone with their fingers.[78]

But the vast majority who answered the surgeon's call were suffering from illness. In that era—long before antibiotic drugs—disease killed far more men than enemy action. As an Iowa soldier noted, dying in that manner had "all of the evils of the battlefield with none of its honors."[79]

Everyone was well aware of this situation. As Crane noted, "We received the news today of the death of one of the men of our Co, as well as one of the strongest. We left him at Cleveland [Tennessee] sick of Lung Fever [pneumonia]. His name was Corporal James Roberts. Very few are killed in battle compared with the no. that die of disease. We have lost some 25 to disease to 6 killed in battle."[80]

Pneumonia killed many men, as did measles, chicken pox, mumps, and whooping cough. But the worst culprit of physical distress—and for many, death—was intestinal disorders. Crane also noted that "Jerome Bowman is quite poorly having never got rid of his Diarrhea."[81] According to some estimates, more than three-quarters of the entire Union army was afflicted with bowel problems at some point each year of the war. The chief reason was bad water. Latrines and stables were often situated too close to water sources such as streams and wells. Bowman was fortunate. He finally recovered and survived to the end of the war. Tens of thousands of his fellow soldiers were not as lucky, dying far from home in their own filth from waterborne diseases such as dysentery and typhoid fever.

> **WORDS IN CONTEXT**
> **minie ball**
> A cone-shaped bullet with a hollow base and three grooves; it expanded slightly when fired to engage the grooves on the shooter's rifle, providing greater distance, velocity, and accuracy.

Looking Back

An Iconic Photo

Probably the best-known family photo of the Civil War belonged to Amos Humiston, who was killed at Gettysburg. There was just one clue to his identity. As Gettysburg historian Diana Loski explains:

> He had been found clutching an ambrotype [photograph] of three children in his hand. The father, knowing that death was near, had taken out the image and looked at it one last time. The story of the dead soldier clasping the photograph soon made headlines. Newspapers and magazines published the picture, hoping to find the identity of the ill-fated man and his three children.
>
> One of the magazines that published the photograph and the sad details of its discovery was *The American Presbyterian*, a small publication with relatively few subscribers. The magazine had one subscriber in Portville, New York. After the woman received the magazine in early November of 1863, and read the wretched story of the dead soldier found in Gettysburg, she recognized the photograph of the three children. They were her neighbors, the Humistons. Philinda Humiston and her three children became famous in their grief. Unable to bring her husband's remains for burial in Portville, Philinda received an invitation to come to Gettysburg. . . . The plight of the Humistons was the dilemma of many thousands, and the people of Gettysburg wanted to help. An orphanage opened in Gettysburg, and Philinda Humiston was offered the position of headmistress. Though not a happy occupation, it nevertheless gave Mrs. Humiston the opportunity to work, and to keep her children with her.

Diana Loski, "A Man's Fate, a Town's Tradition," *Gettysburg Experience*, May 2010. www.the gettysburgexperience.com.

Female Nurses Step Forward

Some wounds and illnesses caused discomfort but not enough to justify separating men from their regiments. Others—especially those involving amputation—required transfer to more permanent hospitals located well behind the front lines. At the start of the war, the male-dominated military medical establishment strongly discouraged the use of female nurses. Many doctors and hospital administrators believed that women could not deal with the horrors of war, even at a safe distance from the battlefield. They also feared what might happen to women who were exposed to a constant stream of male strangers.

The number of casualties quickly exhausted the capacity of the small number of male nurses, many of whom were soldiers with little or no medical training. Thousands of women stepped forward to prove that they were just as capable of dealing with gruesome wounds as any man—and then some. As author Stephen G. Hyslop notes, "Physicians soon came to prefer trained female nurses over their former soldier nurses, who didn't know 'castor oil from a gun rod.' By 1862 official preference was given to female nurses in recruitment, paving the way for nursing to become a legitimate profession for women after the war."[82]

In addition to the typical tasks associated with nurses—administering medicine, changing bandages soaked with blood and pus, and keeping track of the healing process—they had many additional tasks. They cooked and served meals. They wrote letters for men who in many cases were not capable of doing it for themselves. And often they cradled men who were still in their teens or early twenties—many of whom were dying—and badly missed their mothers.

Clara Barton and Louisa May Alcott

Probably the most famous Civil War nurse was Clara Barton, a former teacher who was a patent clerk in Washington, DC, when the war began. She immediately began delivering much-needed supplies to sick and wounded Union soldiers. But she realized that she would be most useful on the battlefield. Her first appearance seemed almost miraculous. As the website of the American Red Cross—which she founded in 1881—notes:

Following the battle of Cedar Mountain in northern Virginia in August 1862, she appeared at a field hospital at midnight with a wagon-load of supplies drawn by a four-mule team. The surgeon on duty, overwhelmed by the human disaster surrounding him, wrote later, "I thought that night if heaven ever sent out a[n] . . . angel, she must be one—her assistance was so timely." Thereafter she was known as the "Angel of the Battlefield."[83]

Barton put to rest the prewar doubts about women's ability to perform on the battlefield. On one occasion she dug a bullet out of a soldier's cheek with her pocket knife. On another she was so close to the fighting that a bullet passed through her sleeve and killed the man she was helping. And as she noted, "I [had to wring] the blood from the bottom of my clothing before I could step, for the weight about my feet."[84]

Another notable nurse, Louisa May Alcott, who later became famous as the author of *Little Women*, described a typical day at Union Hospital in Washington, DC. Rising well before dawn, she flung open the hospital windows—even in the dead of winter—to get some fresh air. "A more perfect pestilence-box than this house I never saw," she noted, "cold, damp, dirty, full of vile odors from wounds, kitchens, wash rooms & stables."[85] One at a time, she tried to make the men as comfortable as possible before going to a hurried and less-than-appealing breakfast— fried beef, salt butter, hardtack, and coffee—for herself.

Then it was back to work, with scarcely a moment to rest. She explained:

Till noon I trot, trot, giving out rations, cutting up food for helpless "boys," washing faces, teaching my attendants how beds are made or floors swept, dressing wounds, taking Dr. FitzPatrick's orders (privately wishing all the time that he would be more gentle with my big babies), dusting tables, sewing bandages, keeping my tray tidy, rushing up & down after pillows, bed linen, sponges, book & directions, till it seems as if I would joyfully pay down all I possess for fifteen minutes rest.[86]

Alcott spent afternoons and evenings serving meals, writing letters for the men, or sending word of their deaths to friends and relatives back home. She also helped the doctors with their rounds and administered daily doses of medicine. Finally at nine o'clock she was done and could tumble gratefully into bed, only to get up eight hours later and start again.

Her consolation—and that of other nurses of both sexes—was that the men they treated were grateful. Walt Whitman wrote to his brother that "the amputated, sick, sometimes dying soldiers cling & cleave to me as it were to a man overboard to a plank, & the perfect content they have if I will remain with them, sit on the side of the cot awhile, some young-sters often, & caress them . . . It is delicious to be the object of so much love & reliance, & to do them such good, soothe & pacify torments of wounds."[87]

A Civil War nurse cares for two wounded Union soldiers. Thousands of women took on the work of nursing during the war, providing comfort and care to injured and dying soldiers.

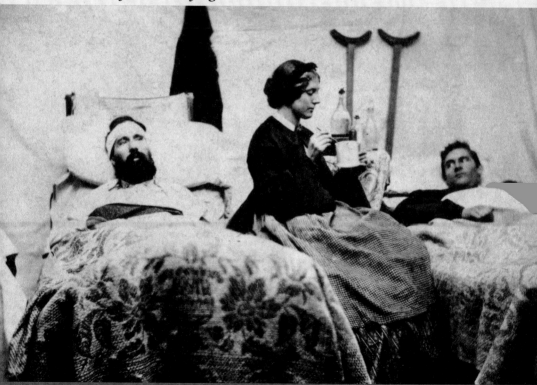

The Sanitary Commission

Nursing was not the only way in which women made major contributions to the welfare of the soldiers. Despite initial opposition from the War Department and Lincoln, a group of concerned, involved women formed the United States Sanitary Commission in May 1861. For political reasons, the top administrators were men, but women—eventually there were several hundred thousand in more than seven thousand local chapters—did virtually all the work.

The Sanitary Commission aided the war effort in several ways, such as improving conditions in hospitals and camps, coordinating donations of food and clothing that poured in from all over the country, setting up "soldiers' homes" where men on leave or on their way to other assignments could stay for free, and even providing stationery and envelopes for men to write letters. While the organization relied heavily on volunteer efforts, it needed money—lots of money—to purchase supplies.

Donations helped raise some of the money. The commission also staged elaborate, multiday fairs in the North's largest cities. For a modest admission fee, fairgoers could attend art exhibits, marvel at spectacular flower arrangements, and admire historical treasures. But mainly they were there to buy food, crafts, paintings, and much more. The first fair, in Chicago in 1863, had a goal of raising $25,000, which skeptics doubted was attainable. They were wrong. Buoyed by the sale of items such as Lincoln's personal copy of the Emancipation Proclamation (which sold for $3,000), the fair pulled in more than $100,000.

There can be little doubt about the effectiveness of the Sanitary Commission. In a typical two-month period in the summer of 1862, the commission furnished nearly two hundred thousand articles of bedding—quilts, blankets, sheets, pillows, pillow cases—to the Army of the Potomac, as well as almost three hundred thousand articles of personal clothing such as shirts, underwear, and socks.

Soldiers' Aid Societies

Less ambitious but no less valuable were hundreds of soldiers' aid societies, which scoured their regions for food, medicine, and money to send to the soldiers. These packages made a huge difference in the living conditions of the soldiers in the field. Socks were especially welcome. The continual marching, which often took place in rain and mud, quickly destroyed socks and left men subject to a variety of debilitating foot ailments. One lucky soldier found a bonus tucked inside his new socks: a note from Ellen M. Sprague of Andover, Connecticut. The note said:

> My dear Friend and brother in our Country's cause: To your care and keeping I commit these socks, and trust they may never be disgraced by any conduct of their wearer. Loyal fingers fashioned them, and may a patriot's tread, whose very step shall tell against our rebel foes, wear them threadbare (if need be) in crushing the wicked rebellion. In every stitch is knit a prayer for our nation's weal, and the hope that peace may smile upon our land long ere these be unfit for use.[88]

Many societies focused on supplying hospitals with needed items such as iron bedsteads and clean sheets. A Sunday school teacher in Maine supplied her unique twist by inscribing her address onto a quilt that she sent to a hospital in Washington, DC. She hoped that the wounded men would correspond with her, thereby encouraging her students to keep sewing. "Your letters would prompt us to more exertions for our patriots,"[89] she wrote.

WORDS IN CONTEXT
weal
What is best for a person or an organization.

For men who often lived for weeks if not months solely in the company of other men, the aid societies could also have another benefit. As George Grenville Benedict of the Twelfth Vermont Infantry noted, "The visit of the Committee of the Ladies of Burlington, Mrs. Dr. Thayer and Mrs. Platt, to our camp yesterday, accompanied by Mrs. Chittenden and Dr. Hatch, was a most agreeable surprise. It was a double pleasure to see faces from home, and *ladies'* faces, which are novelties in camp."[90]

Chapter Five

Black Life in the North: A Different Reality

On the eve of the Civil War, about 4.5 million blacks lived in the United States. About 350,000 were free blacks in the North. Nearly all the rest were slaves working on plantations in the South. At this time the Northern states—many of which had originally allowed slavery—were nearly as restrictive toward blacks as the South. While blacks in the North were no longer enslaved, they encountered significant racial prejudice in a supposedly free society. French author Alexis de Tocqueville, who toured the United States extensively during the early 1830s, noted that

> the Negro [in the North] is free, but he cannot share the rights, pleasures, labors, griefs, or even the tomb of him whose equal he has been declared; there is nowhere where he can meet him, neither in life nor in death. In the South, where slavery still exists, less trouble is taken to keep the Negro apart: they some-times share the labors and the pleasures of the white men; peo-ple are prepared to mix with them to some extent; legislation is more harsh against them, but customs are more tolerant and gentle.[91]

There had been little if any improvement in the condition of Northern blacks since Tocqueville's observations.

A wealthy New York man demonstrated an attitude that was typical of many Northerners toward blacks on the eve of the war when he wrote, "If they were not such a race of braggarts and ruffians I should be sorry for our fire-eating brethren [in the South], weighted down, suffocated and paralyzed by a Nigger incubus four million strong of which no one knows how they are to get rid."[92]

Judging by their actions and their laws, many Northerners acted as if they, too, would like to be rid of the black population. Only four Northern states—Maine, Massachusetts, New Hampshire, and Vermont—allowed blacks to vote. Many did not allow them to attend public schools. Nowhere could they serve on juries. In the years leading up to the war, legislatures in the newer midwestern states enacted so-called Black Laws that either discouraged or forbade blacks from settling there. In Illinois, for example, a black man was guilty of a "high misdemeanor" if he stayed in the state longer than ten days. As a result, blacks made up only about 1 percent of the population of midwestern states.

> **WORDS IN CONTEXT**
> **incubus**
> An evil spirit.

Racism in Indiana

Prejudice toward blacks was especially strong in Indiana. As historian Steven Towne notes, "The racism of the majority whites in Indiana of that era was profound. . . . Many were willing to let Southern whites maintain slavery in the South and keep African-American slave laborers away from their Indiana farms, workshops and homes."[93]

The state's antagonism toward blacks extended even further. As historian Douglas Harper notes, "There was no legal segregation in Indiana's public schools: none was necessary. The white citizens of the state would keep the schools racially pure more thoroughly than any legal provision could. A court upheld the white-only Indiana public schools in 1850, finding that, in the eyes of the state, 'black children were deemed unfit associates of whites, as school companions.'"[94]

Some Indianans took even more extreme positions. During a debate in the state legislature, one man said, "It would be better to kill them [blacks] off at once, if there is no other way to get rid of them. . . . We know how the Puritans did with the Indians, who were infinitely more magnanimous and less impudent than the colored race."[95]

Segregation in the North

In Northern cities most free blacks lived in segregated neighborhoods, at least partly because whites feared that property values would plummet if blacks purchased homes in the areas where they lived. Housing was not the only area of segregation. As history professor Steven F. Lawson notes:

> By the time the Supreme Court ruled in *Dred Scott v. Sanford* (1857) that African Americans were not U.S. citizens, northern whites had excluded blacks from seats on public transportation and barred their entry, except as servants, from most hotels and restaurants. When allowed into auditoriums and theaters, blacks occupied separate sections; they also attended segregated schools. Most churches, too, were segregated.[96]

As a result of this segregation, blacks in the North created social systems that paralleled those of white society—with their own churches, shops, schools, orphanages, and more. Black women in Boston and elsewhere formed soldiers' aid societies similar to the Sanitary Commission and held fairs to raise money and material items for black soldiers. These societies had another purpose that their white sisters took for granted: lobbying for equal treatment and pay for their men in uniform. Other societies helped recently arrived escaped slaves adjust to their new lives. Blacks also established vigilance committees to try to cut down on the violence directed against them. Rampaging groups of Northern whites sometimes descended on black neighborhoods, looting and burning churches, schools, and even private homes.

Black Schooling

One of the most important black social systems dealt with education. Cincinnati, Ohio, had one of the largest concentrations of free blacks in

Freed slaves of various ages attend school during the Civil War. The North was by no means free of racial prejudice but schools provided an important educational, social, and cultural path to advancement that was unattainable in the South.

the North due to its proximity to the South and to the Ohio River, which was a destination for fleeing slaves. The experiences of Cincinnati's black population mirrored those elsewhere. A few years before the war, more than half of the city's black children were enrolled in school. That number dropped to 30 percent after the war began and fell even further over the next four years. There were other handicaps: Even more so than their white counterparts, black youths needed to help their families make ends meet rather than attending school. Whites could attend school beyond the sixth grade, but blacks would not have the same opportunity until after the war.

In most cases the physical conditions of black schools were far worse than white ones. Rats scuttled across the floor of one Cincinnati girls' school in a black neighborhood. A school official noted that another school had to endure an "effluvia which . . . is enough to knock a man to pieces, and make him desire a brandy punch."[97] Holes in the walls of several black schools allowed winter winds to swirl around the rooms. Yet as Vassar College history professor Nikki M. Taylor notes:

> As dilapidated as they were, Cincinnati's public schools were the only buildings outside of the black church that provided a social and cultural space in which to train a new generation of African American teachers, leaders, and administrators. The buildings also provided a space for the transmission of cultural knowledge from teachers to students. Lastly, they were one of only a few public places where African Americans could be together as a community.[98]

Unfavorable Working Conditions

Another significant difference between Northern blacks and whites could be seen in working conditions. Blacks encountered significant opposition to obtaining work, especially in skilled jobs. In Philadelphia, for example, racial prejudice forced many black workers to abandon the trades. The Schomburg Center for Research in Black Culture notes, "The situation in Boston, with its large immigrant population, was even worse."[99]

Former slaves were even more disadvantaged because they had relatively few job skills. Those who did find work often found only menial jobs. Regardless of their origins, blacks were rarely granted the necessary licenses for jobs such as hack drivers or pushcart operators.

In many cases black women found it easier than men to find jobs. There always seemed to be domestic work in the homes of well-to-do whites. Black women also took in laundry and sewing. Many worked for the federal government as cooks, nurses, teachers, and relief workers. Even though they were paid less for comparable work than whites, their employment was often more stable than that of their husbands, and their earnings would become the primary source of support for their families.

WORDS IN CONTEXT

hack

A horse-drawn vehicle used to transport people.

In Their Own Words

The Plight of Educated Blacks

Even for well-educated blacks, life in the North was not easy. As John Rock, a black justice of the peace in Massachusetts—one of the most liberal states in terms of its attitudes toward blacks—noted in 1862:

> The present situation of the colored man is a trying one; trying because the whole nation seems to have entered into a conspiracy to crush him. But few seem to comprehend our position in the free States. The masses seem to think that we are oppressed only in the South. This is a mistake; we are oppressed everywhere in this slavery-cursed land. . . . To be sure, we are seldom insulted by passersby, we have the right of suffrage [voting], the free schools and colleges are opened to our children, and from them come forth young men capable of filling any post of profit or honor. But there is no field for these young men. . . . You can hardly imagine the humiliation and contempt a colored lad must feel by graduating the first in his class, and then being rejected everywhere else because of his color. . . . Nowhere in the United States is the colored man of talent appreciated.

Quoted in J. Matthew Gallman, ed., *The Civil War Chronicle*. New York: Gramercy, 2000, pp. 209–10.

Danger in the Workplace

In Cincinnati one of the relatively few occupations open to blacks was working on steamboats and on the docks along the river. Steamboats were dangerous because boiler explosions were common. Ashore, blacks were given the hardest, dirtiest, most exhausting jobs on the docks. They were often expected to move bales of cotton weighing hundreds of pounds.

The Civil War continued an existing trend in the decline of river traffic. Coupled with an increasing number of freed slaves moving north, this decline resulted in fewer jobs and more people competing for them—creating considerable competition and animosity between whites and blacks for the available jobs. The animosity boiled over in July 1862, when blacks rushed in to take the jobs of Irish and German dockworkers striking for higher wages. Whites retaliated by attacking their replacements. The violence soon spread to black neighborhoods, where blacks with no connection to the strike were beaten and their homes and churches were burned. Some blacks fought back. The violence continued for a week before volunteer troops suppressed it.

Such job-related violence was widespread. In early July 1863 in Buffalo, New York, the *New York Times* noted:

> There was a difficulty between the Irish stevedores [dockworkers] and negroes, this afternoon, in consequence of the former trying to prevent the latter from unloading propellers [propeller-driven ships]. One negro shot an Irishman, it is said, in self-defense, which was the signal for a general onslaught on all the negroes, several of whom are reported killed, and a number severely wounded. Tonight all is quiet, but the longshoremen and stevedores are determined to prevent the negroes from working on the docks.[100]

By far the worst outburst of violence came in New York City a few days later, in response to a newly enacted federal draft law. Angered because blacks (as noncitizens) were exempt from the draft, and fearing loss of jobs, thousands of whites conducted what was the worst rioting the country had ever seen. They overwhelmed the city's police force and controlled the city for nearly four days before being driven back by Union troops. Countless numbers of blacks were beaten. Some were lynched.

An orphanage was burned down, though fortunately none of the children died. More than 120 people, virtually all of them black, perished.

A black man named Charles Jackson almost miraculously avoided being added to the death toll after being attacked. A merchants' committee investigating the riots noted, "His persecutors did not know him nor did they entertain any spite against him beyond the fact that he was a black man. . . Nevertheless they knocked him down, kicked him in the face and ribs, and finally by the hands of their leader, deliberately attempted to cut his throat."[101] Thinking him dead, the mob threw Jackson in the river. Though weakened by blood loss, he swam ashore. Kindly bystanders rescued him and took him to the hospital.

Black laborers build a Union railroad depot stockade for protection against Confederate raids, circa 1863. The work available to freed black slaves was usually exhausting, dirty, and dangerous.

Northern Attitudes Toward Blacks

Northern prejudice against blacks pervaded many areas of daily life. As Valdasta (Georgia) State University history professor David Williams explains:

> The *Christian Recorder* noted that in wartime Philadelphia it was "almost impossible for a respectable colored person to walk the streets without being insulted." The same was true for public transportation. Even a soldier's pass offered Harriet Tubman [a key figure in the Underground Railroad] no protection from abuse. On a train heading home to Auburn, New York, from the Virginia front, she encountered a conductor in New Jersey who was sure her pass was forged or stolen. He could not conceive that a black woman might get such a pass any other way. When Harriet Tubman refused to vacate her seat, four men grabbed her up, dumped her in the baggage car, and there she was held until the train reached Auburn.

David Williams, *A People's History of the Civil War*. New York: New Press, 2005, p. 346.

Black Newspapers

Newspapers were another area in which blacks sought to make their voices heard. According to Dartmouth College professor Colleen Glenney Boggs, "While African-American writers often did not have the same access to writing that their white contemporaries enjoyed, newspapers like the *New York Anglo-African* provided important commentary on the political landscape alongside poetry and fiction."[102] The paper, established in 1859 by two abolitionist black brothers, Thomas and Robert Hamilton, was regarded as the leading black forum in New York City during the Civil War.

Another important paper was Cincinnati's *Colored Citizen*. Established in 1863, its circulation soon spread to other major cities in the region, such as Louisville, Chicago, and Indianapolis, Indiana. Its mission statement read, "Feeling the stern necessity of a medium through which to speak, hear and be heard, to defend the right and denounce wrong, touching our interest more especially in this city, where colored citizens are shamefully wronged, we assume the responsibility of publishing the *Citizen*."[103] Despite glowing accolades from readers, neither paper survived past the end of the war.

Putting on the Blue

Despite having to endure prejudice, violence, and difficult living conditions, many Northern blacks felt as strongly about serving in the military as whites. At its outbreak they were swept up in the same wave of enthusiasm that engulfed the Union. In Philadelphia, for example, an assembly of black men in front of Independence Hall who wanted to enlist could have filled two Union regiments. Hardly anyone paid attention because of the white belief that blacks were unqualified for military service. In early 1862 Frederick Douglass, a former slave who became one of the most eloquent voices advocating freedom for slaves, said, "We are fighting the rebels with one hand, when we ought to be fighting them with both. We are recruiting our troops in the towns and villages of the North, when we ought to be recruiting them on the plantations of the South. . . . We have been catching slaves, instead of arming them."[104] He, too, was ignored.

A few blacks did succeed in joining up in the war's early days. Though he was not officially a soldier, Nicholas Biddle, a sixty-five-year-old former slave, joined his white neighbors in the Pottsville, Pennsylvania, volunteer militia as they headed south. The men marched past a hostile crowd in Baltimore, Maryland. When the mob saw Biddle, they screamed racial epithets. Then an object struck Biddle in the face, deep enough to cut to the bone. He soon returned home. His tombstone reads, "In Memory of Nicholas Biddle, Died August 2, 1876. His was the Proud Distinction of Shedding the First Blood in the Late War for the Union, Being Wounded while Marching through Baltimore with the First Volunteers from Schuylkill County. 18 April 1861. Erected by his Friends in Pottsville."[105]

Differing Viewpoints

Even when blacks were finally allowed to enlist, many Northerners had a low opinion of their value. William T. Sherman, one of the best Northern generals, argued, "Can a negro do our skirmishing and picket duty? Can they improvise bridges, sorties, flank movements, etc., like the white man? *I say no.*"[106] He did, however, feel that they might have some value; they could be "used for some side purposes and not be brigaded with our white men."[107] It did not take long for Union officers to find plenty of "side purposes" for the newly enlisted blacks. They were given jobs as laborers, often doing work such as digging latrines, which whites especially disliked.

> **WORDS IN CONTEXT**
> **picket duty**
> An assignment to patrol a campsite to guard against enemy attack.

Ulysses S. Grant, who later became the top Union general, disagreed with such low assessments of blacks as soldiers. "By arming the Negro we have added a powerful ally. They will make good soldiers and taking them from the enemy weakens him in the same proportion they strengthen us."[108]

The North's black population had several reasons for fighting. Many believed that serving their country in uniform would lead to citizenship, which the *Dred Scott* decision had specifically ruled out. Additionally, many Northern blacks were either former slaves themselves or had relatives who were still enslaved. Being given a gun to use against slaveholders and their supporters provided plenty of motivation.

Louisiana's Best Blood

Eventually, two hundred thousand blacks joined the Union armed forces. It did not take long to demonstrate that Grant and others like him were correct. The process began when General Benjamin Butler, commander of Union forces in Louisiana, urgently requested additional troops to defend New Orleans in late 1862. When his request was turned down, in desperation he formed a regiment of black troops called the Louisiana Native Guard. Most were escaped slaves, though some were free men fathered by members of prominent white families. "Sir, the best blood of Louisiana is in that regiment!"[109] said the regiment's white commander.

A recruitment poster featuring a proud black regiment and its commanding officer urges free blacks and escaped slaves to join the Union army. Black regiments overcame adversity to distinguish themselves as skilled and courageous fighters.

The regiment—and two more formed soon afterward and combined into the Corps d'Afrique—dispelled any doubts about their courage and fighting ability during a frontal assault against well-entrenched Confederate positions at Port Hudson, Louisiana, the following May. More than 150 Native Guards were killed or wounded. Colonel Benjamin H. Grierson, a Union cavalry officer present at the battle, wrote, "There can be no question about the good fighting quality of negroes, hereafter, that question was settled beyond a doubt yesterday."[110]

That "fighting quality" became far more widely known two months later. The Fifty-Fourth Massachusetts, a black regiment, was ordered to attack Fort Wagner. The installation guarded the entrance to Charleston, South Carolina. As George Stephens, a member of the regiment, wrote, "The rebs withheld their fire until we reached within fifty yards of the work, when jets of flame darted forth from every corner and embrasure [door or window]. . . . Some few entered the fort, and when they got in, it was so dark that friends could not be distinguished from foes, and there is no doubt but that many a Union soldier was killed by his comrades."[111] The men could not hold their position and fell back, leaving behind half of their original strength. But as Stephens continued, "It is another evidence that colored soldiers will dare go where any brave man will lead them."[112]

Impressive in Parade

The accomplishments of black soldiers influenced the views of white Northerners. After seeing New York's first black regiment parade through the city in March 1864, Maria Lydig Daly commented in her diary, "They were a fine body of men and had a look of satisfaction in their faces, as though they felt they had gained a right to be more respected. Though I am very little Negrophilish [supportive of Negroes] and would always prefer the commonest white that lives to a Negro, still I could not but feel moved."[113]

The *New York Times* took an even more expansive attitude, noting:

Eight months ago the African race in this City were literally hunted down like wild beasts. . . . Now [they] march in solid platoons . . . to the pealing strains of martial music and are everywhere saluted with waving handkerchiefs, with descending flowers, and with the acclamations and plaudits of countless beholders. . . . It is only by such occasions that we can at all realize the prodigious revolution which the public mind everywhere is experiencing.[114]

Added Dangers

The "revolution" did not extend to every aspect of black soldiering. For starters, black privates were paid ten dollars a month, compared to thirteen dollars for whites. In nearly all cases the men served in all-black regiments under white officers. They also faced a double peril in combat, risking not just being killed or wounded but also being returned to slavery or executed if they were captured. There is considerable evidence that hundreds of black soldiers were massacred after the surrender of Fort Pillow in Tennessee in April 1864. Three months later thousands of Union troops—both black and white—were trapped inside a massive crater at the Battle of Petersburg. Confederate riflemen gunned down many of them. As Confederate officer E.P. Alexander explained:

In fact there were, comparatively, very few Negro prisoners taken that day. It was the first occasion on which any of the [Confederate] Army of Northern Virginia came in contact with Negro troops, & the general feeling of the men toward their employment was very bitter. . . . Some of the Negro prisoners, who were originally allowed to surrender by some soldiers, were afterward shot by others, & there was, without doubt, a great deal of unnecessary killing of them.[115]

Black troops faced other hazards. If they were wounded or fell ill, they often did not receive the same treatment as whites. In general, the least competent doctors were assigned to black regiments. On one occasion a black soldier was accused of faking an illness when he reported to sick call and was bucked and gagged as a punishment. He died the next day. On another occasion, a black patient left a medical tent because he needed to relieve himself. The doctor kicked him viciously, and the man died a few hours later.

White troops were routinely given the most up-to-date weaponry. But even though they faced the same dangers in combat, some black regiments fought with muskets more appropriate for battles half a century earlier. A few officials even wanted to deny them that antiquated armament, insisting that their primary weapon should be pikes.

> **WORDS IN CONTEXT**
> **pikes**
> Long wooden staffs with a sharp steel or iron point.

Sacrifice

Virtually no one in the Union army believed blacks were capable of becoming officers. Yet many whites refused to command black troops. Prejudice was one reason. Fear of Southern retaliation was another. Some Southerners threatened to execute captured white officers commanding black troops. The threats did not end with death. The fate of the body of Colonel Robert Gould Shaw, who led the assault on Fort Wagner, served as a cautionary tale. The Confederates refused the usual battlefield courtesy of returning fallen senior officers. "We have buried him with his niggers,"[116] sniffed one. It was meant as an insult, but it backfired. The phrase became a rallying cry and made Shaw into a national hero. "A soldier's most appropriate burial-place is on the field where he has fallen,"[117] said his father.

The sacrifices of Shaw and all the other dead Union soldiers—both black and white—as well as immense material advantages finally allowed the North to prevail. The war ended in April 1865. The cost had been immense. As Harvard University president Drew Gilpin Faust observes, "Civil War Americans lived the rest of their lives with grief and loss."[118] Soldiers who had survived never forgot their comrades who did not. Relatives of the dead often carried small mementos to remind themselves constantly of their loss. For these people and many others in the North, daily life would never return to the way it had been just four years earlier.

Source Notes

Introduction: Starting with Many Advantages

1. Adam Goodheart, *1861: The Civil War Awakening.* New York: Vintage, 2012, p. 187.
2. Daniel W. Crofts, "Communication Breakdown," *Opinionator* (blog), *New York Times*, May 5, 2011. http://opinionator.blogs.nytimes.com.
3. Michael J. Varhola, *Life in Civil War America.* Cincinnati, OH: Family Tree, 2011, p. 20.

Chapter One: Country Life

4. Quoted in J. Matthew Gallman, ed., *The Civil War Chronicle.* New York: Gramercy, 2000, pp. 244–45.
5. Drew E. VandeCreek, "Economic Development and Labor in Civil War Illinois," Illinois During the Civil War, 2002. http://dig.lib.niu.edu.
6. Walter Gable, "Agriculture in Seneca County in the Mid-1800s," Seneca County, New York, July 2010. www.co.seneca.ny.us.
7. Quoted in American Civil War Voices: Life in a Time of Crisis, "1862 Diary of Isaac Hurlburt, Farmer, Broome County New York," 2012. http://americancivilwarvoices.com.
8. Quoted in *American Civil War Voices: Life in a Time of Crisis,* "1862 Diary of Isaac Hurlburt, Farmer, Broome County New York."
9. Gable, "Agriculture in Seneca County in the Mid-1800s."
10. Nicole Etcheson, *A Generation at War: The Civil War Era in a Northern Community.* Lawrence: University Press of Kansas, 2011, p. 66–67.
11. Gable, "Agriculture in Seneca County in the Mid-1800s."
12. Bowling Green State University Center for Archival Collections, "Researching the Biography of a Civil War Soldier," August 2011. www.bgsu.edu.
13. Bowling Green State University Center for Archival Collections, "Researching the Biography of a Civil War Soldier."

14. Caroline Cowles Richards, *Village Life in America 1852–1872: Including the Period of the American Civil War as Told in the Diary of a School-Girl*. New York: H. Holt, 1913. http://archive.org.

15. David Williams, *A People's History of the Civil War*. New York: New Press, 2005, p. 144.

16. Quoted in Williams, *A People's History of the Civil War*, p. 154.

17. Quoted in Nicole Etcheson, "When the Men Went to War," *Opinionator* (blog), *New York Times*, July 19, 2012. http://opinionator.blogs.nytimes.com.

18. Quoted in Etcheson, "When the Men Went to War."

19. Quoted in Edinborough Press, "Dear Mother." www.edinborough.com.

20. Quoted in Edinborough Press, "Wisconsin Women on the Farm." www.edinborough.com.

21. Robert C. Welch, "A Fight in the Fields: The Impact of the Civil War on Midwestern Agriculture," Iowa State University Center for Agricultural History and Rural Studies. www.history.iastate.edu.

22. Quoted in Edinborough Press, "Wisconsin Women on the Farm."

23. Quoted in Edinborough Press, "Wisconsin Women on the Farm."

24. Quoted in Edinborough Press, "Wisconsin Women on the Farm."

25. Quoted in Kevin Hillstrom and Laurie Collier Hillstrom, *American Civil War Primary Sources*. Farmington Hills, MI: UXL, 2000, p. 21.

26. Quoted in Judith Giesberg, *Army at Home: Women and the Civil War on the Northern Home Front*. Chapel Hill: University of North Carolina Press, 2009, p. 32.

27. Quoted in Gable, "Agriculture in Seneca County in the Mid-1800s."

28. Giesberg, *Army at Home*, p. 40.

Chapter Two: City Life

29. Quoted in David Goldfield, *America Aflame: How the Civil War Created a Nation*. New York: Bloomsbury, 2011, p. 10.

30. Christian McWhirter, *Battle Hymns: The Power and Popularity of Music in the Civil War*. Chapel Hill: University of North Carolina Press, 2012, p. 15.

31. McWhirter, *Battle Hymns*, p. 17.

32. Goldfield, *America Aflame*, p. 301.

33. Goldfield, *America Aflame*, p. 213.

34. Susan C. Lawrence, Kenneth M. Price, and Kenneth J. Winkle, eds., *Civil War Washington*, Center for Digital Research, University of Nebraska–Lincoln. http://civilwardc.org.

35. Quoted in "Streetcars in Washington, DC?," DC pages.com. www.dcpages.com.

36. Lawrence et. al., *Civil War Washington*.

37. Quoted in Gallman, *The Civil War Chronicle*, pp. 280–82.

38. Ed Folsom and Kenneth M. Price, "Walt Whitman," Walt Whitman Archive. http://whitmanarchive.org.

39. Quoted in Social and Architectural History of New York City Tenement Houses, "Earliest Tenements and the Problems." www.map sites.net/gotham.

40. Quoted in Gallman, *The Civil War Chronicle*, p. 372.

41. James M. McPherson, *Battle Cry of Freedom*. New York: Oxford University Press, 1988, p. 447.

42. Edward Pessen, "Builders of the Young Republic," US Department of Labor. www.dol.gov.

43. Quoted in McPherson, *Battle Cry of Freedom*, p. 450.

44. Quoted in Giesberg, *Army at Home*, p. 68.

45. Quoted in James M. McPherson, introduction to *The Most Fearful Ordeal: Original Coverage of the Civil War by Writers and Reporters of the* New York Times. New York: St. Martin's, 2004, p. ix.

46. Quoted in Gallman, *The Civil War Chronicle*, p. 484.

47. Quoted in Williams, *A People's History of the Civil War*, p. 116.

48. Quoted in Williams, *A People's History of the Civil War*, p. 116.

Chapter Three: Building and Sustaining an Army

49. Goodheart, *1861: The Civil War Awakening*, p. 169.

50. Henry W. Tisdale, "Civil War Diary of Sergeant Henry W. Tisdale." www.civilwardiary.net.

51. Quoted in Brooks D. Simpson, Stephen W. Sears, and Aaron Sheehan-Dean, eds., *The Civil War: The First Year Told by Those Who Lived It.* New York: Penguin, 2011, pp. 311–12.

52. Nicole Etcheson, "When the Men Went to War."

53. Teaching with Primary Sources, "Women in the Civil War," Library of Congress. http://library.mtsu.edu.

54. Geoffrey Ward, *The Civil War: An Illustrated History*. New York: Knopf, 1990, p. 50.

55. Quoted in Adam J. Kawa, "No Draft!," *Civil War Times Illustrated*, June 1998, p. 58.

56. Quoted in Ward, *The Civil War*, p. 243.

57. Tisdale, "Civil War Diary of Sergeant Henry W. Tisdale."

58. Quoted in Wayne Phaneuf, "Civil War, October 1862: Bounty Jumpers, Pickpockets and Politicians," *Republican*, October 6, 2012. www.masslive.com.

59. Quoted in Ward, *The Civil War*, p. 50.

60. Quoted in Michael Caruso, *The Ultimate Guide to the Civil War*. Washington, DC: Smithsonian, 2012, p. 17.

61. Quoted in Robert Niepert, "Crimes and Punishments in the Civil War, Part Two: The Sentence Carried Out," Florida Reenactors Online, 2004. www.floridareenactorsonline.

62. Quoted in *Civil War and Northwest Wisconsin* (blog), "1861 September 14: Colonel Paine's Discipline for the Regiment's Drinking and Gambling," September 14, 2011. http://thecivilwarandnorthwest wisconsin.wordpress.com.

63. David Lane, "A Soldier's Diary, The Story of a Volunteer, David Lane, (17th Mich. Vol. Infantry)," Daily Observations from the Civil War. http://dotcw.com.

64. Quoted in Linda Wheeler, "Hardtack Is Easy to Make, Hard to Eat," *Washington Post*, December 12, 2004. www.washingtonpost.com.

65. Quoted in Charles Wright Wills, "Army Life of an Illinois Soldier, Charles Wright Wills, (8th Illinois Infantry)," Daily Observations from the Civil War. http://dotcw.com.

66. Quoted in Ann Crane Salzman Farriar, ed., *Baron Hutchinson Crane: His Civil War Letters*. Parma, OH: privately printed, 2000, p. 37.

67. Josiah Marshall Favill, "Diary of a Young Officer—Josiah Marshall Favill (57th New York Infantry)," Daily Observations from the Civil War. http://dotcw.com.

68. Quoted in Farriar, *Baron Hutchinson Crane*, p. 32.

69. Quoted in Wisconsin Historical Society, "'Old Abe' the Eagle Accompanies the 8th Wisconsin Infantry into War." www.wisconsin history.org.

70. George Grenville Benedict, "Army Life in Virginia by George Grenville Benedict," Daily Observations from the Civil War. http://dotcw.

71. Terry L. Jones, "The Fighting Irish Brigade," *Opinionator* (blog), *New York Times*, December 11, 2012. http://opinionator.blogs.nytimes .com.

Chapter 4: Taking Care of the Troops

72. Andrew F. Sperry, *History of the 33rd Iowa Infantry Regiment: 1863–66*. Des Moines, IA: Mills, 1866, p. 82. http://archive.org.

73. Quoted in Farriar, *Baron Hutchinson Crane*, p. 8.

74. Quoted in John D. Billings, *Hardtack and Coffee: The Unwritten Story of Army Life*, Perseus Digital Library. www.perseus.tufts.edu.

75. George F. Noyes, *The Bivouac and the Battlefield*. New York: Harper and Bros., 1863, p. 21. http://archive.org.

76. Quoted in Mike West, "Minie Balls Were Battlefield Revolution," *Murfreesboro (TN) Post*. www.murfreesboropost.com.

77. Terry L. Jones, "Brother Against Microbe," *Opinionator* (blog), *New York Times*, October 26, 2012. http://opinionator.blogs.nytimes .com.

78. Quoted in David Herbert Donald, ed., *Gone for a Soldier: The Civil War Memoirs of Private Alfred Bellard*. Boston: Little, Brown, 1975, p. 219.

79. Quoted in Drew Gilpin Faust, *This Republic of Suffering: Death and the American Civil War*. New York: Knopf, 2008, p. 4.

80. Quoted in Farriar, *Baron Hutchinson Crane*, p. 20.

81. Quoted in Farriar, *Baron Hutchinson Crane*, p. 20.

82. Stephen G. Hyslop and Neil Kagan, ed., *Eyewitness to the Civil War*. Washington, DC: National Geographic, 2006, p. 348.

83. American Red Cross, "Founder Clara Barton," 2013. www.redcross .org.

84. Quoted in Ward, *The Civil War*, p. 164.

85. Quoted in Gallman, *Civil War Chronicle*, p. 273.

86. Quoted in Gallman, *Civil War Chronicle*, p. 273.

87. Quoted in Gallman, *Civil War Chronicle*, p. 355.

88. Quoted in Matthew Warshauer in ConnecticutHistory.org, "The Complicated Realities of Connecticut and the Civil War." http://connecticuthistory.org.

89. Quoted in Eve M. Kahn, "Stitching Together Civil War History," *New York Times*, June 28, 2012. www.nytimes.com.

90. Benedict, "Army Life in Virginia by George Grenville Benedict."

Chapter Five: Black Life in the North: A Different Reality

91. Alexis de Tocqueville, *Democracy in America*, trans. George Lawrence. New York: Harper Perennial Modern Classics, 2000, p. 246.

92. Quoted in Ward, *The Civil War*, p. 25.

93. Steven Towne, "Emancipation in Indiana," *Opinionator* (blog), *New York Times*, September 27, 2012. http://opinionator.blogs.nytimes.com.

94. Douglas Harper, "Exclusion of Free Blacks," Slavery in the North, 2003. www.slavenorth.com.

95. Quoted in Harper, "Exclusion of Free Blacks."

96. Steven F. Lawson, "Segregation," Freedom's Story, TeacherServe©, National Humanities Center, February 13, 2013. http://nationalhumanitiescenter.org.

97. Quoted in Nikki M. Taylor, *Frontiers of Freedom: Cincinnati's Black Community, 1802–1868*. Athens: Ohio University Press, 2005, p. 170.

98. Taylor, *Frontiers of Freedom*, p. 171.

99. Schomburg Center for Research in Black Culture, "The Northern Migration," In Motion: The African-American Migration Experience. www.inmotionaame.org.

100. Quoted in Harold Holzer and Craig L. Symonds, eds., *The New York Times Complete Civil War*. New York: Black Dog & Leventhal, 2010, p. 253.

101. Quoted in Gallman, *Civil War Chronicle*, pp. 335–36.

102. Colleen Glenney Boggs, "A War of Words," *Opinionator* (blog), *New York Times*, October 2, 2012. http://opinionator.blogs.nytimes.com.

103. Quoted in Taylor, *Frontiers of Freedom*, p. 131.

104. Gallman, *Civil War Chronicle*, p. 136.

105. Quoted in John David Hoptak, "Nicholas Biddle: A Forgotten Hero of the Civil War," *The 48th Pennsylvania Infantry* (blog), February 2, 2007. http://48thpennsylvania.blogspot.com.

106. Quoted in Ward, *The Civil War*, p. 247.

107. Quoted in Williams, *A People's History of the Civil War*, p. 361.

108. Quoted in Ward, *The Civil War*, p. 247.

109. Quoted in Terry L. Jones, "The Free Men of Color Go to War," *Opinionator* (blog), *New York Times*, October 19, 2012. http://opinionator.blogs.nytimes.com.

110. Quoted in Jones, "The Free Men of Color Go to War."

111. Quoted in Gallman, *Civil War Chronicle*, p. 338.

112. Quoted in Gallman, *Civil War Chronicle*, p. 339.

113. Quoted in Gallman, *Civil War Chronicle*, p. 392.

114. Quoted in Gallman, *Civil War Chronicle*, pp. 391–92.

115. Quoted in Gallman, *Civil War Chronicle*, p. 443.

116. Quoted in National Park Service: Civil War Series, "The Civil War's Black Soldiers," March 15, 2011. www.nps.gov.

117. Quoted in National Park Service: Civil War Series, "The Civil War's Black Soldiers."

118. Faust, *This Republic of Suffering*, p. 266.

For Further Research

Books

Nicole Etcheson, *A Generation at War: The Civil War Era in a Northern Community*. Lawrence: University of Kansas Press, 2011.

Drew Gilpin Faust, *The Republic of Suffering: Death and the American Civil War*. New York: Knopf, 2008.

Judith Giesberg, *Army at Home: Women and the Civil War on the Northern Home Front*. Chapel Hill: University of North Carolina Press, 2009.

David Goldfield, *America Aflame: How the Civil War Created a Nation*. New York: Bloomsbury, 2011.

Adam Goodheart, *1861: The Civil War Awakening*. New York: Vintage, 2012.

Harold Holzer and Craig L. Symonds, eds., *The* New York Times *Complete Civil War*. New York: Black Dog & Leventhal, 2010.

Christian McWhirter, *Battle Hymns: The Power and Popularity of Music in the Civil War*. Chapel Hill: University of North Carolina Press, 2012.

Brooks D. Simpson, Stephen W. Sears, and Aaron Sheehan-Dean, eds., *The Civil War: The First Year Told by Those Who Lived It*. New York: Penguin, 2011.

Michael J. Varhola, *Life in Civil War America*. Cincinnati, OH: Family Tree, 2011.

Websites

Civil War Life, Edinborough Press (www.edinborough.com/Learn /Civil_War_Life/Life.html). This website includes first-person accounts of life during the Civil War, stories that people read during this period, Sanitary Fairs, and children's games.

Civil War Diary of Sergeant Henry W. Tisdale (www.civilwardiary .net). An account of nearly three years of life in the Union army, including a lengthy captivity.

Daily Observations from the Civil War (http://dotcw.com). A day-by -day chronicle of the war, told by a wide variety of the people who lived through it.

Disunion (http://opinionator.blogs.nytimes.com/category/disunion). Daily series in the *New York Times* written by respected scholars on the Civil War, with many entries reflecting events that happened on a particular date 150 years ago.

Seneca County Farming During the Civil War Era (www.co.seneca .ny.us/dpt-genserv-historian-seneca.php). A detailed article about a typical New York farm, based on a diary maintained by Henry K. Dey.

Index

93

Picture Credits

About the Author

Jim Whiting has published nearly two hundred nonfiction books for young readers. He has also edited another two hundred titles spanning many genres. His diverse career includes seventeen years publishing *Northwest Runner* magazine, advising a national award-winning high school newspaper, providing hundreds of venue and event descriptions and photography for America Online, serving as sports editor for the *Bainbridge Island Review* in Washington State, and writing hundreds of articles for newspapers and magazines throughout the country. He also coaches middle-school cross country.